IN GOD AMERICAN FOUNDING FATHERS TRUSTED

The Studies Of Construction And Erosion Of American Value System Through The Use Of Quotes Of Founding Fathers And Others

Dipo Toby Alakija

ISBN: 978- 978- 354-217-4

Published In 2019 By
CALVARY ROCK PUBLISHING

19, Ajina Street, Ikenne Remo,
Ogun State, Nigeria.

www.calvaryrock.org

For Christian Education And Ministration Services

INTRODUCTION

The presentations of committee of five of the second continental congress who drafted what would become the Declaration of Independence of July 4th, 1776 announced to the full congress that the thirteen colonies at war with the kingdom of Great Britain are sovereign States. They are, therefore, no longer under British rule.

These States took a collective first step towards forming the United States with the declaration signed by representatives from New Hampshire, Massachusetts Bay, Rhode Island, Connecticut, New York, New Jersey, Pennsylvania, Maryland, Delaware, Virginia, North Carolina, South Carolina and Georgia.

The Founding Fathers of the United States were group of philosophers, politicians and writers who led the American Revolution against the kingdom of Great Britain. Most of them were descendants of colonists who settled in the thirteen colonies of North American.

The term: Founding Fathers which was coined by Warren G Harding is sometimes used to refer to those who signed the embossed version of the Declaration of Independence in 1776. Prior to and during the 19th century, Founding Fathers were simply referred to as the "Fathers" which had been used to describe the founders and first settlers of the original royal colonies.

Apart from other researched materials, speeches and quotes of some of these Founding Fathers and other notable figures in American history and modern days are part of the studies in relation to American Value Systems

THE AMERICAN QUESTS FOR FREEDOM

Going by quotes of some Founding Fathers like Thomas Jefferson who said, *"Occasionally the tree of liberty must be watered with the blood of patriots and tyrants"* and Benjamin Franklin who said, *"They who can give up essential liberty to obtain a little temporary safety deserve neither liberty nor safety"*, and going by their activities especially during The American Revolutionary War between 1775 and 1783, Americans cherished freedom even to the point of death.

The war which is also known as American War of

Independence was between Great Britain and its thirteen colonies.

Patriots who are also known as Revolutionaries, Continentals, Rebels or American Whigs protested against taxation without representation which was followed by Stamp Act; resulting into boycotts. It resulted into conflicts with Sons of Liberty (a secret organization that was created in the thirteen colonies) destroying a shipment of tea on December 16, 1773. Britain responded by closing Boston Harbor and passing a series of The Intolerable Act by the British Parliament in 1774 which is meant to punish the Massachusetts colonies for their defiance in the Tea Party.

Massachusetts colonies responded with Suffolk Resolves which was a declaration made on September 9, 1774 by leaders of Suffolk County, Massachusetts. The declaration rejected the Massachusetts Government Act and resolved to boycott imported goods from Britain unless the Intolerable Acts were repealed.

Massachusetts colonies established a shadow government which wrested control of the country from the Crown.

Twelve colonies formed a Continental Congress to coordinate their resistance, establishing committee and conventions which eventually seized power.

British attempted to disarmed the Massachusetts militia in Concord. This resulted into open combat on April 19, 1775. Militia forces besieged Boston, forcing British evacuation in March 1776, and Congress appointed George Washington who later became the United State first President to command the Continental Army.

The second Continental Congress voted for independence and issued its declaration on July 4th 1776.

What is known as Second War of American Independence was declared on June 18, 1812 when James Madison signed Congress's official declaration of war against England. This is because Great Britain and France which allied with the then thirteen colonies in the war of independence from Great Britain had been at war, off and on since 1793. The United States which traded with both countries was caught in the middle with Britain blocking all French seaports and insisted that US ships first stop at British port and pay a fee before continuing to France.

Secondly, Britain was also interfering in the affairs of Canada, America's neighbor.

The war of 1812 which came to be known as the second American war of independence was fought on land and on the sea and lasted almost three years. One of the biggest offensives was the British attack on the capital city of Washington D C.

The British soldiers landed on the East Coast on August 19, 1814, and stormed Washington on August 24. The 63-year old Madison barely escaped captured as British soldiers burned Washington, including White House and the Capitol building.

The United States and Britain each won several important battles until they eventually grew tired of warfare and signed a peace treaty in Belgium on December 24, 1814. The treaty recognized previous existing boundaries between American and British territory.

While he was held aboard a British ship that bombed Baltimore's Fort McHenry through the night on the morning of September 14, 1814, Francis Scott Key was inspired to write a poem that began: "O say can you see..?". He could not believe that the Fort's flag was still flying. Key thought his poem should be sung to an English melody called "To Anacreon In Heaven."

After the war, the poem and music were united and first published in Philadelphia as the "Star Spangled Banner". It was then played on patriotic occasions.

In 1889, the secretary of the Navy ordered the song to be played each time the flag was raised.

Congress did not pass a law making the "Star Spangled Banner" the National Anthem until 1931.

Through "Star Spangled Banner", the United States is able to get its motto: "In God We Trust."

The Nation Anthem goes as follows:

O! say can you see, by the dawn's early light,
What so proudly we hailed at the twilight's last gleaming,
Whose broad stripes and bright stars through the perilous fight,
O'er the ramparts we watched, were so gallantly streaming?
And the rockets' red glare, the bombs bursting in air,
Gave proof through the night that our flag was still there;

O! say does that star-spangled banner yet wave
O'er the land of the free and the home of the brave?

On the shore dimly seen through the mists of the deep,
Where the foe's haughty host in dread silence reposes,
What is that which the breeze, o'er the towering steep,
As it fitfully blows, half conceals, half discloses?
Now it catches the gleam of the morning's first beam,
In full glory reflected now shines in the stream:
'Tis the star-spangled banner, O! long may it wave
O'er the land of the free and the home of the brave.

And where is that band who so vauntingly swore
That the havoc of war and the battle's confusion,
A home and a country, should leave us no more?
Their blood has washed out their foul footsteps' pollution.
No refuge could save the hireling and slave
From the terror of flight, or the gloom of the grave:
And the star-spangled banner in triumph doth wave,
O'er the land of the free and the home of the brave.

O! thus be it ever, when freemen shall stand
Between their loved homes and the war's desolation.
Blest with vict'ry and peace, may the Heav'n rescued land
Praise the Power that hath made and preserved us a nation!
Then conquer we must, when our cause it is just,
And this be our motto: 'In God is our trust.'
And the star-spangled banner in triumph shall wave
O'er the land of the free and the home of the brave

BRIEF HISTORICAL BACKGROUNDS OF THE AMERICAN FOUNDING FATHERS

According to Roger Sherman, the Founding Fathers represented a cross-section of 18th-century U. S. leadership. According to a study of the biographies by Caroline Robbins, the Signers of the Declaration of Independence came for the most part from an educated elite, were residents of older settlements, and belonged with a few exceptions to a moderately well-to-do class representing only a fraction of the population. Native or born overseas, they were of British stock and of the Protestant faith.

4

Almost all of them were leaders in their communities. Many were also prominent in national affairs. Virtually every one had taken part in the American Revolution; at least 29 had served in the Continental Army, most of them in positions of command.

Many of the Founding Fathers attended or held degrees from the colonial colleges, most notably Columbia known at the time as "King's College", Princeton originally known as "The College of New Jersey", Harvard College, the College of William and Mary, Yale College and University of Pennsylvania. Some had previously been home schooled or obtained early instruction from private tutors or academies. Others had studied abroad. Ironically, Benjamin Franklin who had little formal education himself would ultimately establish the College of Philadelphia based on European models.

With a limited number of professional schools established in the U. S., Founders also sought advanced degrees from traditional institutions in England and Scotland such as the University of Edinburgh, the University of St. Andrews, and the University of Glasgow.

The Founding Fathers practiced a wide range of high and middle-status occupations, and many pursued more than one career simultaneously. They did not differ dramatically from the Loyalists, except they were generally younger and less senior in their professions.

Historian Caroline Robbins in 1977 examined the status of the Signers of the Declaration of Independence and concluded: There were indeed disparities of wealth, earned or inherited: some Signers were rich, others had about enough to enable them to attend Congress.... The majority of revolutionaries were from moderately well-to-do or average income brackets. Twice as many Loyalists belonged to the wealthiest echelon. But some Signers were rich; few, indigent.... The Signers were elected not for wealth or rank so much as because of the evidence they had already evinced of willingness for public service. A few of them were wealthy or had financial resources that ranged from good to excellent, but there are other founders who were less than wealthy.

THE FOUNDATION OF AMERICAN VALUE SYSTEM

Research works reveal that the founding fathers directly or indirectly quoted the Bible four times more than other source. Without God, the Bible, the constitution, the enlightenment; the United States would not have been so unique. In other words, America was founded on faith in God.

Calvin Coolidge, the 30th President of the United States said, *"The foundations of our society and our government rest so much on the teachings of the Bible that it would be difficult to support them if faith in these teachings would cease to practically universal in our country."*

Ronald Regan, the 40th President of the United States said, *"Of the many influences that shaped the United States into a distinctive nation and people, none may be said to be more fundamental and enduring than the Bible."*

Franklin T. Lambert (2003) has examined the religious affiliations and beliefs of some of the Founders. Of the 55 delegates to the 1787 Constitutional Convention, 28 were Anglicans (in the Church of England; or Episcopalian, after the American Revolutionary War was won), 21 were Protestants, and two were Roman Catholics (D. Carroll, and Fitzsimons). Among the Protestant delegates to the Constitutional Convention, eight were Presbyterians, seven were Congregationalists, two were Lutherans, two were Dutch Reformed, and two were Methodists.

What is essential to note in these research works is that most of the Founding Fathers, especially the Presidents were Christians or raised as Christians. Based on this fact and going by quotes of some Founding Fathers and earliest Presidents, it is save to conclude that American Value System is constructed with Christian values and virtues. The issue to now address is the belief in God, which will possibly give reasons for their convictions.

THE BELIEF IN GOD

The item in the book titled: Insanity Of Humanity, written by the same author is extracted for studies which may provide insights under the question of the belief in God.

It goes as follows:

There is an argument in a classroom between a Christian student and a professor of philosophy who is a diehard

6

Atheist. Unlike in some arguments that are scripted by agents of mind control to sway the minds of audience to their side, this argument is based on science, information and sound opinions. The story goes like this.

The Professor of philosophy said to his students in the class, "let me explain the problem science has with Jesus Christ." The atheist professor paused before he looked at one of his new students. He told him to stand up. "You're a Christian, aren't you, son?"

"Yes, sir," the student replied. "Absolutely."

"Is God good?" the professor asked.

"Sure! God is good, and I will keep the faith."

"Is God all powerful? Can God do anything?"

"Yes."

"Are you good or evil?"

"The Bible says I'm evil."

The professor grinned knowingly. "Aha! The Bible!" He thought for a moment. "Here is one for you. Let's say there's a sick person over there and you can cure him. You can do it. Would you help him? Would you try?"

"Yes, sir, I would," the student replied.

"So you're good...!"

"I wouldn't say that."

"But why not say that? You'll help a sick and maimed person if you could. Most of us would if we could. But God doesn't."

The student did not answer. So the professor continued, "God doesn't, does he? My brother was a Christian who died of cancer, even though he prayed to Jesus to heal him. How is this Jesus good? Hmmm? Can you answer that one?"

The student remained silent.

"No, you can't, can you?" the professor asked. He took a sip of water from a glass on his desk to give the student time to relax. "let's start again, young fella. Is God good?"

"Er... Yes, "the student says.

"Is Satan good?"

The student did not hesitate to answer, "no"

"Then where does Satan comes from?"

The student faltered, "from.... God..."

"That's right," the professor said gleefully." God made Satan, didn't he? Tell me, son. Is there evil in this world?"

"Yes, sir."

"Evil is everywhere, isn't it? And God did make everything, correct?"

"Yes, sir."

"So who created evil?"

Again, the student has no answer.

"Is there sickness? Immorality? Hatred? Ugliness? All these terrible things. Do they exist in this world?"

The student squirmed on his feet, "yes."

"So who created them?"

The student did not answer again. So the professor repeated his question, "who created them?"

There is still no answer. Suddenly the lecturer broke away to pace in front of the classroom. The class was mesmerized. "Tell me," he continued, apparently enjoying himself. "Do you believe in Jesus Christ, son?"

The student's voice betrayed him and cracked, "yes, professor, I do."

The professor stopped pacing. "Science says you five senses, you use to identify and observe the world round you. Have you ever seen Jesus?"

"No, sir, I've never seen Him."

"Then tell us if you've ever heard your Jesus?"

"Perhaps not, sir."

"Have you ever felt your Jesus, tasted your Jesus or smelt your Jesus? Have you ever had any sensory perception of Jesus Christ or God for that matter?"

"Perhaps not."

"Yet you still believe in him?"

"Yes."

"According to the rules of empirical, testable, demonstrable protocol, science says your God doesn't exist. What do you say to that, son?"

"Nothing," the student replied. "I only have my faith."

"Yes, faith," the professor repeated. "And that is the problem science has with God. There is no evidence, only faith."

The student stood quietly for a moment before asking a question of his own. "Professor, is there such thing as heat?"

"Yes," the professor replied. "There is heat."

"And is there such a thing as cold?"

"Yes, son. There is cold too."

"No, sir, there isn't."

The professor turned to face the student. He was obviously interested. The room suddenly became very quiet. The student began to explain. "You can have lots of heat, even more heat, super heat, mega-heat, white heat, a little heat or no heat, but we don't have anything called a cold. We can hit 458 degrees below zero, which is no heat, but you can't go any further after that. There is no such thing as cold; otherwise we would be able to go colder than 458 degrees. You see, sir, cold is only a word we used to describe the absence of heat. We cannot measure cold but we can measure heat in thermal units because heat is energy. Cold is not the opposite of heat, sir, just the absence of it."

There was complete silence across the room. A pen drops somewhere in the classroom, sounding like a hammer.

"What about darkness, professor? Is there such a thing as darkness?"

"Yes," the professor replied without hesitation. "What is night if it isn't darkness?"

"You're wrong again, sir. Darkness is not something. It is absence of something. You can have low light, normal light, bright light, flashing light... but if you have no light constantly you have nothing and it's called darkness, isn't it? That's the meaning we use to define the word. In reality, darkness doesn't exist. If it does, you would be able to make darkness darker, wouldn't you?"

The professor began to smile at the student. He thought this would be a good semester.

He asked, "so what point are you making, young man?"

"Yes, professor. My point is, your philosophical premise is flawed to start with and so your conclusion must be flawed."

The professor could not hide his surprise this time.

"Flawed? Can you explain how?"

"You are working on the premise of duality." the student explained. "You argue that there is life and there's death, a good God and a bad God. You are viewing the concept of God as something we can measure. Sir, science can't even explain a thought. It uses electricity and magnetism, but has never seen, much less fully understood either one. To view death as opposite of life is to be ignorant of the fact that death cannot exists as a substantive thing. Death is not the

opposite of life, just the absence of it. Now tell me, professor. Do you teach your students that they evolved from a monkey?"

"If you are referring to the natural evolutionary process, young man, yes, of course, I do."

"Have you ever observed evolution with your own eyes, sir?"

The professor began to shake his head, still smiling, as he realized the trend of the argument - a very good semester indeed.

"Since no one has ever observed the process of evolution at work and cannot even prove that this process is an on-going endeavor, are you not teaching your own opinion, sir? Are you not now a scientist, but a preacher?"

The class went gaga with uproar. The student remained silent until the commotion subsided.

"To continue the point you were making earlier, let me give you an example of what I mean?" the student said, looking around the room. "Is there anyone in the class who has ever seen the professor's brain?"

The class burst into laughter.

"Is there anyone here who has ever heard the professor's brain, felt the professor's brain, touched or smelt the professor's brain? No one appeared to have done so. So, according to the established rules of empirical, testable, demonstrable protocol, science says that you have no brain, with all due respect, sir. So if science says you have no brain, how can we trust your lectures, sir?"

Now the room was dead silent. The professor just stared at the student, his face unreadable.

Finally, after what seemed an eternity, the professor answered, "I guess you'll have to take them to faith."

That ended the argument. The class knew who won.

THE AMERICAN VALUE SYSTEM

Going by the motto: *In God We Trust*, derived from the National Anthem and going by quotes of some Founding Fathers who later became earliest Presidents like George Washington; John Adams and Thomas Jefferson, the American Value System is confirmed to be based on the Bible to a very large extent.

George Washington, the first President said, *"It is impossible to rightly govern a nation without God and the Bible."*

John Adams, the second President said, *"We recognize no sovereign but God and no king but Jesus!"*

Thomas Jefferson, the third President said, *"The reason that Christianity is the best friend of government is because Christianity is the only religion that changes the heart."*

Many other quotes of the Founding Fathers and other Presidents are also confirmations that the American Value System is built on strong faith in God. The departure from this strong faith in God probably accounted for the bloody civil war in the United States between 1861 and 1865, going by what Abraham Lincoln who was the 16th President at that time observed. He said, *"We have forgotten God. We have forgotten the gracious hand, which preserved us in peace and multiplied and enrich and strengthened us, and we have vainly imagined, in the deceitfulness of our hearts, that these blessings were produced by some superior wisdom and virtue of our own. Intoxicated with unbroken success, we have become too self-sufficient to feel the necessity of redeeming and preserving grace, too proud to pray to the God that made us."*

What Abraham Lincoln was able to achieve through his faith in God that was demonstrated during the civil war and the analysis of his quote gives vivid pictures of the consequences of losing faith or forgetting God.

These include but not limited to the followings:

1. Anyone or any nation that forgets God or the knowledge of His Word would be forgotten by God. Anyone who is forgotten by God will get into trouble. Thus Patrick Henry, 1st and 6th Governor Of Virginia said, *"It is when people forget God that tyrants forge their chains."* This is also confirmed in Hosea 4:6-9, which says, *"My people are destroyed for lack of knowledge: because thou hast rejected knowledge, I will also reject thee, that thou shalt be no priest to me: seeing thou hast forgotten the law of thy God, I will also forget thy children. As they were increased, so they sinned against me: therefore will I change their glory into shame. They eat up the sin of my people, and they set their heart on their iniquity. And there shall be, like*

people, like priest: and I will punish them for their ways, and reward them their doings." Perhaps this is the reason Ronald Wilson Regan, the 40th President said, "If we ever forget that we are one nation under God, then we will be under."

2. The peace that is enjoyed at the time of keeping faith in God would be lost if God is left out of anything or everything about life. Thus, no matter what anyone or nation may be going through, if the person or the leadership does not lose faith in God, he or she will overcome the situation just as Abraham Lincoln was able to lead the United States out of civil war. George Washington confirmed this fact when he said, "The propitious smiles of heaven can never be expected on a nation that disregards the eternal rules of order and right, which heaven itself has ordained."

3. For anyone or nation to lose faith in God is to fill the hearts with vanities and deceitfulness. This is confirmed in the Bible in Corinthians 3:18 to 20, which says, "Let no man deceive himself. If any man among you seems to be wise in this world, let him become a fool, that he may be wise. For the wisdom of this world is foolishness with God. For it is written, He takes the wise in their own craftiness. And again, The Lord knows the thoughts of the wise, that they are vain."

4. Pride which is destructive is the end result of anyone or any nation that fails to attribute its success to God.

In the final analysis of Abraham Lincoln's quote, it must be noted that those who stand with God in faith will always have God doing things for them which they cannot do for themselves. This is confirmed in the book of Romans 8:31 in the Bible, which says, "What shall we then say to these things? If God be for us, who can be against us?"

THE CONSTRUCTION OF AMERICAN VALUE SYSTEM

Just like the construction of a house, there are materials which are used to construct the Value System of a nation.

Values can be explained as set of beliefs that are prevailing in a particular area and among a group of people. Value System can be described as the means or platforms of impacting or enforcing the beliefs which form the norms and cultures of a particular group of people. It is usually handed

12

over by one generation to another. The value system often reflects what the group or society stands for or stand against. They are usually built up when couples come together and raise families, which grow into extended families and much later into communities. Groups of communities grow into a state or nation.

There are various values identified in the United States through studies of quotations of the Founding Fathers and other materials. They are:

(1) FAMILY VALUES: These are sets of beliefs within a nuclear or extended family, often enforced or influenced by the leaders like parents or grandparents. Thus if there is any issue arising among members of the same family, they are usually resolved by the family leader, based on the family values. Samuel Adams, one of the signers of Declaration of Independence said in his letter to Thomas Well, *"Religion in a family is at once its brightest ornament and its best security."*

(2) TRADITIONAL VALUES: These are sets of beliefs prevailing within all groups of families in a particular community, usually enforced or influenced by the community leaders. Thomas Jefferson said to Thomas Lomax in February 25, 1801, *"If we can once more get social intercourse restored to its pristine harmony, I shall believe we have not lived in vain."*

(3) RELIGIOUS VALUES: These are set of beliefs within a particular religious institution or organization, guarded by religious or other leaders. Grover Cleveland, the 22nd President said, *"All must admit that the reception of the teaching of Christ results in the purest patriotism in the most scrupulous fidelity to public trust, and in the best type of citizenship."*

(4) NATIONAL VALUES: These are sets of beliefs, which are codified laws and order. Benjamin Franklin, one of the founding fathers said, *"Freedom is not a gift bestowed upon us by other men, but a right that belongs of God and nature."* James Madison said, *"Do not separate text from historical background. If you do, you will have perverted and subverted the constitution, which can only end in a distorted, bastardized form of illegitimate government. "*

Based on studies, the American Value System was firmly constructed by the founding fathers on faith in God. For this reason, the motto remains *"In God We Trust"* till today.

The following items are common in all the four types of in American Value Systems:

(1) Respect for laws, norms and order. Disrespect always attract sanction or punishment either by the law or leader. Thus when James Madison saw the need to make people respect law and order, he said, *"If men were angels, no government would be necessary."* Even leaders are mandated to have respect for law. Thus Theodore Roosevelt, 26th President said, *"No man is above the law and no man is below it: nor do we ask any man's permission when we ask him to obey it."*

(2) Preservation of rights and freedom of the people. This is established in the quote of John Adams who said, *"you will never know how much it has cost my generation to preserve your freedom. I hope you will make good use of it."* For this reason, there is usually enforcement of law and order. The type of punishment to be imposed on anyone who contravenes the law and order depends on how much the family, the community or the nation needs to discourage the offence.

(3) American Value Systems are usually designed to promote peace, unity, harmony and good relationship among community and family members and also among fellow citizens of the nation. Thomas Paine, said, *"If there must be trouble, let it be in my days, that my child may have peace."* Thomas Jefferson added, *"Educate and inform the whole mass of the people. Enable them to see that it is in their interest to preserve peace and order, and they will preserve them."* George Washington exploded, *"To be prepared for war is one of the most effectual means of preserving peace."* War in this context does not necessarily means invasion of other countries but rather war against anything that threatens the peace and unity of all the states in the United States.

The entire American Value System was so well designed and constructed by the Founding Fathers that it became the life wire that powers other machineries. Once this system breaks down, other sectors like the security, economy, social and political systems begin to malfunction or get shut down. If, however, the Value System is in order, every member of the society will recognize his or her role, making everybody and everything to fit into all other systems or structures.

DEFAULTS IN THE AMERICAN VALUE SYSTEM

With the foundation upon which the American Value System is built, the nation is expected to be a role model if not to all but to most nations in the entire world. Instead of serving as a role model, however, a lot of other nations are hostile towards the United State in the modern days. Results of research works indicate that there are defaults in the Value System which accounted for high rate of crimes, giving basis for the hostilities of some nations against the United States.

The analysis of various quotes of some founding members who were sound philosophers like Thomas Jefferson, the 3rd President give deep insight into the causes of the defaults in the Value System.

Thomas Jefferson was well-learned in the fields of religion and philosophy. He authored the Virginia Statue for Religious Freedom which serve as a precursor to the Establishment Clause and Free Exercise Clause. His ideologies are perceived as progressive, deep and very relevant till the present age.

According to results of research works, the followings are identified as causes of series of defaults in the American Value System:

(I) Legislation That Are Opposed To The Value System
(II) Faulty Economic Policies
(III) Cult Religions And Satanism In The Society
(IV) Faulty External And Internal Affair Policies

Before considering the above as the causes of the defaults in the Value System, there is need to first identify and study the hallmarks of the sound leadership of the founding fathers who actually constructed it with their ideologies and religion.

Their quotes and studies of their lives, especially the earliest Presidents establish the followings as hallmarks of their sound and committed leadership:

1. *Religious Convictions:* Toping the list of the hallmarks of the leadership of the founding fathers is their faith in Jesus

Christ. In fact, of all the 56 men who signed the Declaration of Independence, almost half of them had been through seminaries or Bible schools. Most notably, all the earliest Presidents of the United States were fond of quoting the Bible. John Quincy Adams, the 6th President of the United States said, *"My custom is to read four or five chapters of the Bible every morning immediately after rising. It seems to me the most suitable manner of beginning the day. It is an invaluable and inexhaustible mine of knowledge and virtue."* James Madison, the 4th President said, *"We have staked the whole future of American civilization not on the power of Government, far from it. We have staked the whole of our political institution upon the capacity of mankind of self-government, upon the capacity of each and all of us to govern ourselves according to the commandments of God. The future and success of America is not in this constitution, but in the laws of God upon which this constitution is founded."* Going by these and several other quotes, the earliest American leadership was characterized with strong religious convictions. The founding fathers must have witnessed or perceived the proofs of the move of God on their side. They must also have had proper understanding of the Bible passage in Hebrew 11:6 that says, *"But without faith it is impossible to please him: for he that comes to God must believe that he is, and that he is a rewarder of them that diligently seek him."*

Faith in God, according to historical facts, brought about the followings in America during the struggle for and after independence:

(A) It gave the people the courage to struggle and the hope for independence from the British because faith in God brings about fear of God and fear of God removes fear of man. Thus George Washington said before the battle of Long Island in August 26, 1776, *"The fate of the unborn millions will now depend, under God, on the courage and conduct of the army."* The prayer in Psalm 56:1 to 7 of Bible must have been applied. It says, *"Be merciful unto me, O God: for man would swallow me up; he fighting daily oppresses me. Mine enemies would daily swallow me up: for they be many that fight against me, O thou most High. What time I am afraid, I will trust in thee. In*

16

God I will praise his word, in God I have put my trust; I will not fear what flesh can do unto me. Every day they wrest my words: all their thoughts are against me for evil. They gather themselves together, they hide themselves, they mark my steps, when they wait for my soul. Shall they escape by iniquity? in thine anger cast down the people, O God."

(B) Faith in God which brought about principles of unity and love made it possible for the people to cooperate with one another in building the United States into vibrant nation. John Adams wrote on June 28, 1813 to Thomas Jefferson, *"The general principles, on which the fathers achieve independence were the only principles in which that beautiful Assembly of young Gentlemen could unite, and these principles only could be intended by them in their address, or by me in my answer. And what were these general principles? I answer, the general principles of Christianity, in which all these sects were united..."* In confirmation to that, the Bible says in Ephesians 4:13 to 16, *"Till we all come in the unity of the faith, and of the knowledge of the Son of God, unto a perfect man, unto the measure of the stature of the fulness of Christ: That we henceforth be no more children, tossed to and fro, and carried about with every wind of doctrine, by the sleight of men, and cunning craftiness, whereby they lie in wait to deceive; But speaking the truth in love, may grow up into him in all things, which is the head, even Christ: From whom the whole body fitly joined together and compacted by that which every joint supplies, according to the effectual working in the measure of every part, makes increase of the body unto the edifying of itself in love."*

(C) Preservation of peace, laws and order was made possible through teachings in the Bible, according to some of the founding fathers. John Adams said, *"suppose a nation in some distant region should take the Bible for their only law book, and every member should regulate his conduct by the precepts exhibited! Every member would be obliged in conscience, to temperance, frugality, and industry; to justice, kindness, and charity towards his fellow men, and to piety, love,*

17

and reverence toward Almighty God... What a Eutopia, what a paradise this region be." The Bible confirms this claim in Psalm 119:165 which says, *"Great peace have they which love thy law: and nothing shall offend them."* Thomas Jefferson said, *"Educate and inform the whole mass of the people. Enable them to see that it is their interest to preserve peace and order, and they will preserve them."*

(D) The founding fathers' faith in God gave them outstanding wisdom and understanding with which they laid a solid foundation of the American Value System. Dr. Benjamin Bush, one of the signers of the Declaration of Independence said, *"The Gospel of Jesus Christ prescribes the wisest rules for just conduct in every situation of life. Happy they who are enabled to obey them in all situations!"* This wisdom and understanding can be compared with none. The Bible establishes this fact in Prover 9:10, which says, *"The fear of the LORD is the beginning of wisdom: and the knowledge of the holy is understanding."*

(E) The founding fathers believed in God for protections and other miracles. George Washington said, *"God's hand was on me. God protected me and kept me through the battle."* Their faith in God worked out for them as it worked out for the blind men in Matthew 9:28 to 29 of the Bible. It says, *"And when he (Jesus) was come into the house, the blind men came to him: and Jesus saith unto them, Believe ye that I am able to do this? They said unto him, Yea, Lord. Then touched he their eyes, saying, According to your faith be it unto you."*

(F) The trust in God as in the quotes of the founding fathers and the motto of the United States brought about blessings of God, unprecedented successes and fulfillment of their desires and endeavors. The Bible confirms this in Psalm 37:3 to 5 which says, *"Trust in the LORD, and do good; so shalt thou dwell in the land, and verily thou shalt be fed. Delight thyself also in the LORD; and he shall give thee the desires of thine heart. Commit thy way unto the LORD; trust also in him; and he shall bring it to pass."*

(G) And most importantly, faith in God makes the founding

fathers conscious of the life in eternity. Samuel Adams, one of the signers of Declaration of Independence said in his Last Will and Testament, *"Principally, and first of all, I resign my soul to the Almighty Being who gave it, and my body I commit to the dust, relying on the merits of Jesus Christ for the pardon of my sins."* Judging by their quotes and lifestyles, the founding fathers knew about the life in eternity probably through the studies of following items in the Bible: *(i) "And as it is appointed unto men once to die, but after this the judgment..."* (Hebrew 9:27) *(ii) "For the wages of sin is death; but the gift of God is eternal life through Jesus Christ our Lord."* (Romans 6:23) *(iii) "But the fearful, and unbelieving, and the abominable, and murderers, and whoremongers, and sorcerers, and idolaters, and all liars, shall have their part in the lake which burns with fire and brimstone: which is the second death."* Revelation 21:8.

2. *Virtuous And Courageous Leadership:* George Washington who possessed outstanding leadership, which probably earned him the position of the first President of the United States said, *"While we are zealously performing the duties of good citizens and soldiers, we certainly ought not to be inattentive to the higher duties of religion. To the distinguished character of a Patriot, it should be our highest glory to add the more distinguished character of a Christian."* Thomas Jefferson said, *"I am a real Christian, that is to say, a disciple of the doctrines of Jesus. I have little doubt that our whole country will soon be rallied to the unity of our Creator and, I hope, to the pure doctrine of Jesus."*

Because the foundation of the American Value System is based on the teachings of the Bible, going by their activities and founding fathers' quotes, some of the Christian characteristics which are explained in 2 Peter 1: 5 to 10 were apparent in their styles of leadership. The passage says, *"And beside this, giving all diligence, add to your faith virtue; and to virtue knowledge; And to knowledge temperance; and to temperance patience; and to patience godliness; And to godliness brotherly kindness; and to brotherly kindness charity. For if these things be in you, and abound, they make you that you shall neither be barren nor unfruitful in the knowledge of our Lord Jesus Christ. But he that lacks these things is blind, and cannot see afar off, and hath forgotten that he was purged from his old sins. Wherefore the rather, brethren, give diligence to make your calling and election sure: for if ye do these things, ye shall never fall..."*

These characteristics include the followings:

(A) Diligence in the service of God by serving the people. Thomas Jefferson said, *"The price of freedom is eternal vigilance."* The Bible says in 2 Corinthians 8: 7 to 9, *"Therefore, as ye abound in every thing, in faith, and utterance, and knowledge, and in all diligence, and in your love to us, see that ye abound in this grace also. I speak not by commandment, but by occasion of the forwardness of others, and to prove the sincerity of your love. For ye know the grace of our Lord Jesus Christ, that, though he was rich, yet for your sakes he became poor, that ye through his poverty might be rich."*

(B) Faith in God and faithfulness in His service to the people. Thomas Jefferson said, *"God who gave us life gave us liberty. And can the liberties of a nation be thought secure when we have removed their only firm basis, a conviction in the minds of the people that these liberties are of the gift of God? That they are not to be violated but with His wrath? Indeed, I tremble for my country when I reflect that God is just; that His justice cannot sleep forever..."* The Bible says in Hebrew 6:10 to 12, *"For God is not unrighteous to forget your work and labour of love, which ye have shewed toward his name, in that ye have ministered to the saints, and do minister. And we desire that every one of you do shew the same diligence to the full assurance of hope unto the end: That ye be not slothful, but followers of them who through faith and patience inherit the promises."*

(C) Christian virtues which are developed through reading the Bible. It says in 2 Corinthians 3:2-3. *"You are our epistle written in our hearts, known and read of all men: Forasmuch as ye are manifestly declared to be the epistle of Christ ministered by us, written not with ink, but with the Spirit of the living God; not in tables of stone, but in fleshy tables of the heart."* George Washington said, *"A good moral character is first essential in a man.... It is therefore highly important that you should endeavor not only to be learned but virtuous."*

(D) Leaders' knowledge of the word of God. The Bible says in Proverb 2:3 to 6 *"Yea, if thou cries after knowledge, and lifts up thy voice for understanding; If thou seeks her as silver, and searches for her as for hid treasures; Then shalt thou understand the fear of the LORD, and find the knowledge of God. For the LORD giveth wisdom: out of his mouth cometh knowledge and understanding."* The United States Congress assembled and recommended an edition of the Bible to the inhabitants of the United States in 1782, saying, *"... A neat edition of the Holy Scriptures for the use of schools."*

(E) Temperance, which can be explained as the ability to control onself and impulses. This ability is part of law that guide leaders against misdeeds. The Bible says in Galatians 5:23, *"... Meekness, temperance: against such there is no law."* Thomas Jefferson said, *"When angry count to ten before you speak. If very angry, count to on hundred."*

(F) Patience of leadership, especially in fulfilling its aims and objectives. Benjamin Franklin said, *"Genius is nothing but a greater aptitude for patience."* The Bible says in Isaiah 28:16, *"Therefore thus saith the Lord GOD, Behold, I lay in Zion for a foundation a stone, a tried stone, a precious corner stone, a sure foundation: he that believeth shall not make haste."*

(G) Leadership Godliness. It can be described as Christ-like or righteousness or right-standing with God. The Bible says in Proverb 14:34 *"Righteousness exalts a nation: but sin is a reproach to any people."* James Madison said, *"Cursed be all that learning that is contrary to the cross of Christ."* The Bible again says in 1st Timothy 2:2 *"For kings, and for all that are in authority; that we may lead a quiet and peaceable life in all godliness and honesty."*

(H) Brotherly kindness. It is for the people at various levels, including leaders to care for one and another. This often invokes spirit of patriotism. One of the major things that characterized the earliest leadership in the United States, especially during and after the struggle for independence is spirit of patriotism. The founding fathers were so possessed with this spirit that they formed a group of patriots. The Bible says in Matthew 22:37 to 40 *"Jesus said unto him, Thou shalt love the Lord thy God with all thy heart, and with all thy soul, and with all thy mind. This is the first and great commandment. And the second is like unto it, Thou shalt love thy neighbour as thyself. On these two commandments hang all the law and the prophets."* Through feelings of love and brotherly kindness for the people, the leaders were able to identify the feelings and the needs of the people. True love of the leaders makes them less concerned about their own safety, caring more for the general good. William Ellery, one of the signers Declaration of Independence said, *"We look forward to the time when power of love will replace the love of power. Then will our world know the blessing of peace."*

(I) Charity has to do with selfless services, loving and caring for one another. This often begins with leadership. George Washington said, *"I was summoned by my country, whose voice I can never hear but with veneration and love."*

Legislation That Are Opposed To The Value system

America is blessed with sound and spiritually matured founding fathers who laid very good political and other foundations for the coming generations to build on. Thus Calvin Coolidge, the 30th President of the United States said, *"our government rests upon religion. It is from that source that we derive our reverence for truth and justice, for equality and liberality, and for the rights of mankind. Unless the people believe in these principles they cannot believe in our governments. There are only two main theories of government. One rests on righteousness and the other on force. One appeals to reasons, and the other to the sword. One exemplified in the republic, the other is represented by despotism....*

"The government of a country never gets ahead of the religion of a country. There is no way by which we can substitute the authority of law for the virtue of man. Of course we endeavor to restrain the vicious, and furnish a fair degree

of security and protection by legislation and police control, but the real reform which society in these days is seeking will come as a result of our religious convictions, or they will not come at all. Peace, justice, humanity, charity - these cannot be legislated into being. They are the result of divine grace. "

The 30th President's quote highlighted his observations on how things had been going wrong in his days. The points, which undermine the American Value System, are as follow:

(A) The foundation of American Systems, including politics rest heavily on Christian religion. This had been pointed out in the quotes of the founding fathers. Andrew Jackson said, *"The Bible is the rock on which the republic rests."* On June 25, 1962, however, the United States Court decided in Engel v. Vitale that a prayer approved by New York Board of Regents for use in schools violated the First Amendment because it represents establishment religion. George Washington prayed, *"Oh, eternal and everlasting God, direct my thoughts, words and work. Wash away my sins in the immaculate blood of the Lamb and purge my heart by Thy Holy Spirit. Daily, frame me more and more in the likeness of Thy Son, Jesus Christ, that living in Thy fear, and dying in Thy favor, I may in Thy appointed time obtain the resurrection of the justified unto eternal life. Bless, O Lord, the whole race of mankind and let the world be filled with the knowledge of Thee and Thy Son, Jesus Christ."*

(B) Establishing truths and justice are based on Biblical principles, going by the quotes of the founding fathers. Patrick Henry, Ratifier of the U. S. Constitution said, *"It cannot be emphasized too often that this great nation was founded, not by religionists, but by Christians; not on religions, but on the gospel of Jesus Christ. For this very reason peoples of other faiths have been afforded asylum, prosperity, and freedom of worship here."* Truth and justice which are sometimes made complicated to establish by modern legislation are crucial in all the machineries, including the value system of every nation for the following reasons:

1. Without truth, there would be miscarriage of justice. James Wilson said, *"... Opinions... upon every other*

subject, ought to be founded in truth. Justice, as well as truth, requires... accuracy and impartiality of opinion." And if there is injustice, there would be social disorder. Thomas Jefferson said, *"When injustice becomes law, resistance becomes duty."* The Bible says in 1 Thessalonians 5:21, *"Prove all things; hold fast that which is good."*

2. Without truth, criminal will appear innocent while innocent people will appear like criminals. The Bible says in Proverb 29:12, *"if a ruler hearken to lies, all his servants are wicked."* What makes a ruler who listens to lies wicked can be found in the fact that if criminals are allowed to go away with their crimes, the entire society will be under threats, making the environment tensed and hostile. Similarly, if innocent people are punished for the offence they have not committed, the ruler would be considered by the Bible as being wicked.

3. Without truth, leaders would deceive the followers and may appoint or select or elect wrong people into leadership or sensitive positions. John Basil Barnhill said, *"When the people fear the government there is tyranny, when the government fears the people there is liberty."* The Bible says in Psalm 89:14, *"Justice and judgment are the habitation of thy throne: mercy and truth shall go before thy face."*

4. Without truth, including the state of the nation either economically or politically or in other things, the country cannot make progress. Going by research works, the truth in what Thomas Jefferson said is often neglected in the American legislation that relates to national debt. He said, *"It is incumbent of every generation to pay its own debt as it goes. A principle which if acted on would save the one-half the wars of the world."* So as at 2019, the US has accumulated more than $21 trillion as national debt.

5. Without truth, leaders and citizens will be misinformed, making the country to be deformed. Thomas Jefferson said, *"It is error alone which need the support of the government. Truth can stand by itself."* The Bible says in Jeremiah 9:3, *"And they bend their tongues like their bow for lies: but they are not valiant for the truth upon*

the earth; for they proceed from evil to evil, and they know not me, saith the LORD." In order words, lies can bring about catastrophes in the society.

(C) Lives and properties cannot be secured and protected by legislation and police control, according to what is noted in Calvin Coolidge's in his quote. The people can be secured and protected through building everyone, especially children and youths into responsible and reasonable citizens by boosting their moral values. This can only be done through teaching them values since, as pointed out, the National Value System is the live-wire that powers every other machineries in the society; including the economic and political structures.

(D) Promotion of equality and liberality within the society. Since American Value System is based on moral principles in the Bible, the founding fathers expected the coming generations to safeguard it with the use of legislation. Through that, there would be promotion of equality and liberality among the citizens. The Bible says in 2 Corinthians 8:13 to 14, *"For I mean not that other men be eased, and ye burdened: But by an equality, that now at this time your abundance may be a supply for their want, that their abundance also may be a supply for your want: that there may be equality..."*

So many unscrupulous ideas that seriously undermine the American value system, however, have infiltrated the society in the name of freedom. The principles that once make the United States a society of Christian virtues are threatened with extinction, creating a society of ungodliness and violence. The methods through which unscrupulous ideas infiltrated the society need to be studied before anyone can make attempt to influence the required change in the society.

They are as follow:

(A) *Teaching Method:* This is a way of using schools and Colleges to impact wrong ideas into young minds. The following excerpt is made from the book: Insanity Of Humanity: *"Rick Santorum revealed that American colleges brainwash students, making home schooling more important in the present days.*

Raymond Houghton said, "...absolute behaviour control is imminent."

25

According to analysts, conforming the masses to a particular way of thinking requires all the sophisticated tools and tactics which had been developed at the various "behavioural science research institutes. Education laboratories were established first in England, then in the Soviet Union and Nazi Germany, and finally in the United States. Going by the battles of these psycho-social engineers against an unsuspecting public, they would "wash" away individual thinking, free speech and all the other rights of Americans and other people in the world. The vacuum would be filled with lofty ideals, enticing images and deceptive promises designed to mold minds that match their global vision. Group thinking and other controls and incentives would enforce compliance..."

What is instructive to note is that educationists and academic book writers are in the positions to shape the psyches of the nation through schools and books, especially that of young minds. It is indicated in the prologue in one of author's play books titled: "Bloodshed In Campus" which is the result of research works on cultism on Nigerian campus, *"now is the age when literary and academic works must point out vices and their repercussions in our society."* Subjects like Moral Instructions which is going into extinctions need to be brought back into the education system, using stories like the ones the author designed to boost children's moral values with titles: Foundation Bible Club, Young Generation Story books and others. A lot of children's story books which authored by globalists and cultists are designed to celebrate vices, crimes or magic. If magical fantasies are created in the minds of children instead of realities, they may be lured into occultism or rituals.

(B) *Conduct Method:* This method is done through what people, especially children and youths observe in the environments that are created for them by adults like parents, teachers and other people in the position of influence. Just like other human beings, young ones have eyes to watch the conduct of parents or teachers. They have the memory to record what they see and they have other parts of the brain that use the information to act.

All humans have both beasts and saints in them. Thus if people, particularly young ones are exposed to violent conduct of adults like domestic violence, the beasts in them are easily made active. If they are exposed to environments of peace; love and tolerance, the saints in them are made active. Thomas Paine said, *"If there must be trouble, let it be in my day, that my child may have peace."* One of the ways there can be peace in future is not to encourage or celebrate violence but to campaign against it in every way. In the book by the same author with the title: Spoil The Child, Destroy The Nation, the following is an excerpt of the dialogue in one of the dramas titled: Beast In The Child:

(Mandy and Oyekoya are in the sitting room with fruit drinks in front of them, sitting beside each other.)

MANDY: *... As you know, I lived for almost ten years in the US. My father always insisted that I marry a Nigerian like my family. I didn't really know why until I was given a topic to research on in the College. The topic is: Causes Of Violence In The United States. The research work exposed me to a lot of materials that stunned me. I first started by reading a book titled: "Pawn In The Game", written by a researcher called William Guy Carr, born in 1895 and died in 1959. (She shrugs.) The guy was considered a conspiracy theorist but he seemed to have firm grip over historical facts. I was so impressed by the findings of this researcher that I memorize some parts of the book. It says, "if what I reveal surprises and shocks the readers, please, don't develop an inferiority complex because I am frank to admit that although I have worked since 1911, trying to find out why human race can't live in peace... It was in 1950 before I penetrated the secret that the wars and revolutions which scourge our lives, and chaotic conditions that prevail, are nothing more or less than the effect of the Luciferian conspiracy...*

OYEKOYA: *(frowns.) What does that mean?*

MANDY: *It means it was the idea of Lucifer, the falling*

angel that is causing a lot of bloodshed in the world, giving people reasons to go into war.

OYEKOYA: (looks a little amused.) B-but what has that got to do with the toys I gave to my son?

MANDY: It has a lot to do with it but I will use the case of a three year old boy I came across in the course of the research work to explain. The boy had been so brainwashed with toy guns and other weapons of violence that he did not know the difference between real ones and the toy version. One day, while his mother was at the shopping mall, the boy was told to stay with her things, including her handbag. He opened the handbag and found a gun inside. You know a lady's gun... (She gestures with her right hand.) It's a small and very handy gun. You can imagine how small it is if a boy could grip and balance it in his hands. He aimed it at his mother and pulled the trigger just as you have it with toy guns. He shot her dead!

OYEKOYA: (looks stunned.) What? Why?

MANDY: It's simple. The boy thought the gun was a toy. (Oyekoya looks thoughtful.) According to the result of my research works on the causes of violence in the United States, children are made familiar with violence through toys, computer games and movies, including cartoons.

OYEKOYA: This is hard to believe, Mandy.

MANDY: Yeah, you're telling me. But it is true. There are several cases like that. The US Police always make it look like accidents.

OYEKOYA: B-but… Why would anyone want to create a violent society?

MANDY: You don't want us to go into that part, do you...?

(C) <u>Entertainment Method</u>: This method is a way of passing a message through entertainments like music, movies, story books etc. What most people do not realize about this method is that it is the most effective method of passing messages whether negative or positive. Many American citizens are being programmed with wrong set of values through movies and music. This excerpt which explains how the brain respond to entertainments is also taken from the book: Insanity Of Humanity: *"Experiments conducted by researcher Herbert Krugman reveals that when a person watches television, brain activity switches from the left to the right hemisphere. The left hemisphere is the seat of logical thought. This is where information is broken down into its component parts and critically analyzed. The right brain, however, treats incoming data uncritically, processing information in wholes, leading to emotional, rather than logical responses. The shift from left to right brain activity also causes the release of endorphin, body's natural opiates - thus it is possible to become physically addicted to watching television, a hypothesis borne out of numerous studies which has shown that very few people are able to kick the television habit. It is no longer an overstatement to note that most youths today that are raised and taught through network television are intellectually dead by their early teens.*

The dumbing down of humanity is represented by another shift which occurs in the brain when we watch television. Activity in the higher brain regions (such as the neo-cortex) is diminished, while activity system increases. The latter, commonly referred to as the reptile brain, is associated with more primitive mental functions, such as the "fight" or "fright" response. The reptile brain is unable to distinguish between reality and the pretended reality of television. To the reptile brain, if it looks real, it is real. Thus, though we know on a conscious level that it is "only a film," and yet, for instance, the heart beats faster while we watch a suspenseful scene. Similarly, we know the commercial is trying to manipulate us, but on an unconscious level, the commercial nonetheless succeeds in, say, making us feel inadequate until we buy whatever is being advertised. The effect is all the more powerful because it is unconscious, operating on the deepest level of human response. The reptile brain, however, makes it possible for us to survive as biological beings, but it also leaves people vulnerable to the manipulations of television programmers. This is where the manipulators use our own emotions as strings to control us. The distortions and directions we are being moved to are taking place in the subconscious, often undetected....

(D) *Information Method:* This method is a way of sharing facts that is often backed with proofs like pictures and items. This has to do with the use of the media. Results of research works indicate that the media which has become a powerful tool in modern day is now being used to brainwash the masses in most nations all over the world, including the United States. Here is another excerpt from the book: Insanity Of Humanity:

Edward Hunter, author of "Brainwashing in Red China" said in 1958 before a US congressional House committee, "since man began, he has tried to influence other men or women to his way of thinking. There have always been these forms of pressure to change attitudes. We discovered in the past thirty years, a technique to influence by clinical, hospital procedures, the thinking processes of human beings. Brainwashing is formed out of a set of different elements... hunger, fatigue, tenseness, threats, violence, and in more intense cases drugs and hypnotism."

The act of Brainwashing and mind control can be performed in various ways with various means, ranging from trauma to monarch mind control but this chapter will only treat the ways of mass mind control and mild or subtle brainwashing. The mass media is the most powerful tool used by the controlling class to hypnotize or manipulate the masses. It shapes and molds opinions and attitudes. They are designed to reach the largest audience possible. They include the use of television, music, movies, radio, newspapers, magazines, books, records, video games and the internet. Many studies have been conducted in the past century to measure the effects of mass media on the population in order to discover the best techniques to enhance it. From these studies emerged the Science of Communication which is used in marketing, public relations and politics.

According to analysts, there are a growing number of people waking up to the reality of our growing transparent soft cage. There seems to be just enough people who choose to remain asleep. Worse yet, there are even those who were at least partially awake at one time but found it necessary to return to the slumber of dreamland, which is created by the mass media.

One of the most common examples of mind control with the use of media in America, being our case study, is the so-called "free and civilized society" in the advent and usage of television set. Although, of course, this does not mean that everything on TV is geared towards brainwashing or mind control but most of the programming on television today all over the world is run and programmed by the largest media corporations that have interests in defense contracts such as CBS, NBC, FOX and a host of others. This makes perfect sense when you see how slanted and warped the news is today. When the conflicts of interest are examined, it would be discovered that the issue is only viewed at a glance. To understand the multiple ways how lies become truths, you only need to examine the techniques of brainwashing, which the network are employing.

Radio is not different in the ability to brainwash a population into submission. About sixty-seven years ago, six million Americans became unwitting subjects in an experiment in psychological warfare. It was the night before Halloween in 1938. At 8 p.m CST, the Mercury Radio on the Air began broadcasting Orson Welles' radio adaptation of H.G Wells' War Of The Worlds. The story was presented as if it were breaking news, with bulletins so realistic that an estimated one million people believed the world was actually under attack by Martians. Of that number, thousands succumbed to outright panic, not waiting to hear Welles' explanation at the end of the program that it had all been a Halloween prank, but fleeing into the night to escape the alien invaders.

Psychologist Hadley Cantril in his book: The Invasion From Mars: A Study In The Psychology Of Panic, explored the power of broadcast media, particularly as it relates to the suggestibility of human beings under the influence of fear. Cantril was affiliated with Princeton University's Radio Research project, which was funded in 1937 by the Rockefeller Foundation. Also affiliated *with the project was Council on Foreign Relations (CFR) member and Columbia Broadcasting System (CBS) Executive Frank Stanton. Station was the chairman of the board of Rand Corporation, the influential think tank which has done ground breaking research on, among other things, mass brainwashing. With Rockefeller Foundation money, Cantril established the Office of Public Opinion Research (OPOR). Among the studies conducted by OPOR was an analysis of the effectiveness of "psycho-political operations" (which means propaganda in plain English) Of office of Strategic Services (OSS), the forerunner of the Central Intelligence Agency (CIA). During world war 2, Cantril with Rockefeller's money assisted CFR member and CBS reporter Edward R Murrow in setting up Princeton radio propaganda Listening Centre with the purpose of studying Nazi radio propaganda with the object of applying Nazi techniques to OSS propaganda. Out of this project came a new government agency called Foreign Intelligence Service (FBIS). The FBIS eventually became the United State Information Agency (USIA), which is the propaganda arm of the National Security Council. Thus, by the end of the 1940s, the basic research had been done and the propaganda apparatus of the national security state had been set up just in time for the Dawn of Television.*

The above are the commonest methods wrong set of values infiltrated the American society and undermine the value system.

Faulty Economic Policies

As at the early history of the United States, it was a nation of farmers. Agricultural laborers took ninety percent of its workforce in 1790 and around one-fouth as at 1920. Thomas Jefferson attributed the struggle for independence to planters who were hardworking and self sufficient enough to make ideal citizens.

Along with freedom and property rights, America's colonial economy thrived on the brutal system of slavery, with farmers from New York to Georgia relying on free slave labor to produce cotton, tobacco and other crops. When the federal government outlawed slave trade in 1808, as James Madison, the 4th President wrote to Congress, *"it had failed to stamp it out completely. The issue of slave trade which was still legal in Southern states eventually resulted into civil war in the United States."*

Going by historical facts, battles including revolutionary and civil wars are always very expensive to fight. Thus the newly created nation of the United States needed to fund its economic expansion and make good on unpaid Revolution War debts incurred by individual states. Paying them off was politically fraught, however, since federal plan would reward spectators and favor Northern states over Southern states. George Washington chose the divisive "assumption" program proposed by his Treasury Secretary. U. S. Bonds were soon selling in Europe at a premium because they were considered safe.

The history of central banking in the United States began with the charter of The Bank of the United States in February 25, 1791 by the US Congress, signed by President George Washington. It was modeled after the Bank of England, the British Central Bank. The Bank met with considerate controversy. Agrarian interests were opposed to the Bank of the United States because they feared it would favor commercial and industrial interests over their own, and it would promote the use of paper currency at the expense of gold and silver specie. Ownership of the Bank was also another issue. By the time the Bank's charter was up for renewal in 1811, about 70 percent of its stock was owned by foreigners. Although foreign stock had no voting power to influence the Bank's operations, outstanding shares carried 8.4 percent dividend. Another twenty year charter, it was argued, would result in about $12 million in already scarce gold and silver being exported to the Bank's foreign owners.

Thomas Jefferson who was then Secretary of State believed the bank was unconstitutional because it was an unauthorized extension of federal power. Jefferson argued that Congress possessed only delegated powers which were specifically enumerated in the constitution. The only possible source of authority to charter the Bank, Jefferson believed, was in the necessary and proper clause as in Act 1

33

Sec. 8, cl.18.

History continues to prove that economy and politics are interwoven. In fact anyone with economic powers can control politics, going by all the cases that are studied so far. Hence, in 1933, the then U. S Vice President John Garner, when referring to the International Bankers, said, *"You see, gentlemen who owns the United States..."* Baron Nathan Mayer Rothschild, the London based financier, one of the founders of the International Rothschild Banking Dynasty who was born in 1777 and died in 1836 said, *"I care not what puppet is placed on the throne of England to rule the Empire... The man that controls Britain's money supply controls the British Empire. And I control the money supply."*

The question to be addressed now is the reason some founding fathers and a few of the presidents were so intimidated by the powers of central banks to the extent that Andrew Jackson, the 7th President saw the need *"to kill the bank"*? Why is it so important for him to kill the central bank? The simple answer is found in what he achieved when he eventually killed the central bank. He became the only U. S president who ever paid the debt of the nation. Other Presidents like Abraham Lincoln (16th President) and John Fitzgerald Kennedy (35th President) who attempted to do similar thing were both assassinated.

All these historical facts only point out to the issue of power of American central banking.

It has been established that about 70 percent of the Bank of the United States was owned by foreigners. It performed both public and private functions. The most important public function was to control the money supply by regulating the amount of notes state banks could issue, and by transferring reserves to different parts of the country.

The Bank of the U. S. which was also a profit seeking institution competed with the state banks for deposits and loaning customers. Because the Bank was both setting the rules and competing in the marketplace especially irritated state banks. This made them joined with agrarian interests and Jeffersonians in opposition to the Bank.

The power of the Bank was what provoked Andrew Jackson, the 7th President to announce in 1833 that the government would no longer use the central banking known as Second Bank of the United States. He used his executive power to remove all federal funds from the Bank in the final Salvo of what is referred to as the "Bank War." When he was asked about his greatest accomplishment during his two terms as President, he said, *"I killed the bank."* An attempt was made to assassinate the President, which he blamed on some politicians. History seemed to repeat itself in the tenure of Abraham Lincoln, the 16th President who was assassinated in 1865. According to an article titled: "The Rothschild International Plot To Kill Lincoln", published in October 29, 1976 in New Solidarity, Abraham Lincoln was killed as a result of his monetary policies. This theory indicated that Lincoln needed money to finance the Civil War. The Bankers in Europe led by Rothschild offered him loans with high interest rates. Rather than to accept the loans, Lincoln found another means to fund the war effort. More importantly, the British Bankers opposed his protectionist policies. Some Englishmen in the 1860s believed that *"British free trade, industrial monopoly and human slavery travel together."* Lincoln's policies after the civil war would have destroyed the Rothschild's commodity speculations. After the war, Lincoln planned a mild Reconstruction policy which would have enabled a resumption of agriculture production. The Rothschild were betting the other way on high prices, caused by a tough Reconstruction policy toward the South. Lincoln was viewed as a threat to the established order of things, and he was assassinated as a result. The goal was to weaken the United States so the Rothschild could take over its economy.

Considering and comparing similar things in the above article with what happened during Andrew Jackson's war against the Bank, it is save to conclude that the power of central banking is very hard if not impossible for the executive power to contend with.

Using the *"Bank War"* as a case study, when on October 1st 1833, President Andrew Jackson succeeded in withdrawing government fund from the Second Bank of the United States to the state banks, Nicholas Biddle who was the head of the Second Bank threatened, *"nothing but widespread suffering will produce any effect on the Congress... Our only safety is in pursuing a steady course of firm restriction and I have no doubt that such course will ultimately lead to restoration of the currency and re-charter of the Bank."* True to his words, Biddle began calling in old loans, refusing to extend new ones. He made money so scarce that the country began to enter depression. Of course, he blamed the President for crashing the economy. When the President won the war in April 1834 with the house of representatives voting 134 to 82 against re-charter of the Bank, a committee was set up to investigate if the Bank actually caused the crash. Biddle did not allow the investigating committee into the Bank. In January 8, 1835, Andrew Jackson paid off the final instalment of the national debt. Nicholas Biddle was arrested and accused of fraud which confirmed Thomas Jefferson's suspicion of banking fraud when he said in a letter to John Taylor in 1816, *"And I sincerely believe, with you, that banking establishment are more dangerous that standing armies; and the principle of spending money to be paid by posterity, under the name of funding is swindling futurity on a large scale."* Just as in the latter case of Abraham Lincoln, Richard Lawrence attempted to assassinate President Andrew Jackson.

The next intruding case to be considered is the assassination of John Fitzgerald Kennedy (JFK), the 35th President. Ten days before his assassination, he said at Columbia University, *"The high office of President has been used to foment a plot to destroy the American's freedom, and before I leave office I must inform the citizens of his plight."*

With this quote as part of background information, there is need to study the article of Patrick J. Kiger titled: "The Federal Reserve Did It."

Before the study of this article, it is important to note that the history of central banking in the United States does not begin with the Federal Reserve when it first received its charter in February 25, 1791.

Kiger writes as follows:

"A lot of people are deeply suspicious of the Federal Reserve System, which tinkers with interest rates and availability of money to lend stability of the US economy. Or at least, that's what the Trilateral Commission, the Knights Templar and the Masonic elders want us to think....

"So it is not too surprising the conspiracy theorists would

posit that the Fed had a role in JFK's murder as well. Some have suggested JFK ran afoul of the central bankers by issuing Executive Order 11110 in June 1963, which would have taken away the Fed's power to allow the US Treasury to bypass it and issue paper currency backed by silver. This supposedly would have eliminated the demand for federal notes but vastly reduced the U. S. national debt....

"For one thing, silver certificates, as such paper currency was called, already existed. For another, JFK actually wanted to get rid of silver certificates, and had just signed a bill passed by Congress that allowed the government to melt down its silver reserves and use the metal to make coins. To ease the transition, JFK issued the executive order in question, which allowed the government to keep printing certificates for a while longer...."

This article obviously traces assassination of JFK to Federal Reserve. Considering the fact that the US Treasury was in the process of issuing currency before the assassination and barely five months after the death of the President, they were removed and never to be reissued establishes the basis of suspicion. Secondly, considering the cases of Presidents Andrew Jackson and Abraham Lincoln who also had issues with central banking, the suspicion becomes stronger. And also there is this quote of Franklin D. Roosevelt, the 32nd President in a letter to Edward M. House, dated November 23, 1933, saying, "The real truth of the matter is, and you and I know, that a financial element in the large centers has owned the government of the U. S since the days of Andrew Jackson."

After considering the faulty economic policies of the United States, Thomas Jefferson made this prediction which is dawning on American citizens till date: "If American people ever allow private banks to control the issue of their money, first by inflation and then by deflation, the banks and corporations that will grow around them will deprive the people of their property until their children will wake up homeless on the continent their fathers conquered."

The effects of faulty economic policies of the United States are worse than what was predicted. It not only affects American citizens but also the entire world economy. According to the results of various research works, the

37

followings are the effects of faulty economic policies of the United States:

(A) The social and welfare structures are so affected that there are security challenges. Whenever the peace or lives or families or properties of the people are under threats, they naturally react to the threats just like the days of Andrew Jackson when the Bank caused the crash in the economy of the United States.

The power to control the economy more often than not influences the state of the nation. That is the reason the founding fathers took the issue of the economy very seriously. Since this power is too much to be trusted with anyone or group of people, it must be given back to the people. Going by Thomas Jefferson's economic ideologies, true capitalism gives people the power to run the economy of the nation through the federal government instead of centering it on banks or corporations that are owned by individuals. By giving this power to banks, it brings about defaults in social and welfare structures. According to researched works in many countries, including African nations, if there are economic problems at anytime, there would be serious defaults in social and welfare structures in the nation. This invariably cause governments at every level unable to meet up to all their responsibilities to the citizens.

(B) The value system is easily shut down by economic problems, going by cases of different nations that are studied. The shutting down of the value system of a nation creates rooms for bribery and corruption in the public service, making money politics as means to get elected into public offices and causing the crime rate in the society to be on the increase. Once crimes are on the increase, lives and properties may be so unsecured that people may be forced to take up arms in order to protect themselves or their properties. No matter the moral lessons young ones are being taught in schools or at homes, one should expect little or no effect on them if their environments are characterized with sufferings, vices and crimes. Thus it is safe to conclude that any government that is not responsible breed societies of irresponsible citizens just as rogue parents breed rogue children. The rogues that were born the day before yesterday are the causes of the vices of yesterday in any society. The ones that are born yesterday are the causes of the vices of today. The ones that are born today are the ones that will cause the vices of tomorrow with the adverse effects on the nation. Anyone who denies these facts about the state of most nations all over the world may be thinking like a sick man who claims to be healthy instead of seeing the doctor until the sickness either knocks him down or terminates his life.

(C) With the shutting down of the value system by faulty economic policies, the education system which is the brain development of the nation would be tampered with. This often gives rooms for different school lessons and ideas like socialism which are opposed to what the founding fathers stood for to infiltrate the system. One of the cases that are studied is culled from the book: Insanity Of Humanity. It is as follows:

A well known story which bombards children with mind-changing suggestions was narrated to first-graders in America. It typically illustrates both the tactics and the planned transformation of the world.

The story is about the little Red Hen who wanted to eat some bread. She asked some of her barnyard friends to help her in making it. The cat, the dog and the goat all said, "no". She decided to do all the work herself. When the bread was done, its fragrance spread through out the farm; her neighbors who were unwilling to bake the bread with her were willing to help her eat it.

"Wont you share with us?" they begged.

"No," the Red Hen said. "Since you didn't help you don't get anything."

In the context of traditional values, the moral lesson in the story is clear: you get nothing from what you don't work for. The story is intended to promote active work and discourage laziness. But those who have learned to think and see from the new global view are led to a different conclusion. The kinds of questions the first grade teacher asks her class is: "why was the little Red Hen so stingy? Isn't it only right that everyone gets to eat? Why wouldn't she share what she had with some who had none?"

The concerned mother who heard and reported this story

asked, "what kind of values were the children taught?"

The obvious answer to this question of the mother is children were being taught socialist values. The teacher's question was actually strategic suggestions, prompting the group to ridicule traditional values, to see reality and society from the new politically correct perspective, and to shame anyone who dare to disagree.

The educational establishment knows that children who are fed with traditional values or biblical principles will resist the plans for change. The system recognizes the fact that students bombarded with strategic suggestions and idealized images will likely reject Christianity and other values. If schools can build the right kind of framework of filter in the minds of children early enough, the new global beliefs will fit right in. In other words, the battle for the hearts and minds of children will be won by the side that first trains them to see reality from its point of view.

Cult Religions And Satanism In The Society

One of the major things that drastically shut down the American Value System is the introduction of Cult Religions and Satanism into the society right from childhoods of the citizens up to the leadership level. According to the results of research works that are compiled in another of the author's book titled: Satanism And Cult Religions, Satanism had been mingled with Christianity. The introduction of the book is as follows:

"The International Tribunal into Crimes of Church and State (ITCCS) was founded in May, 2010 at a closed door meetings of survivors of Church and State terror in Dublin, Ireland. The event was initiated by Reverend Kevin Annet, a Nobel Price Nominee and member of Irish survivors' group.

"The main purpose of ITCCS is to unite survivors of genocide and child torture across borders and to mount a broad political, spiritual and legal movement to disestablish the Vatican and other Churches and governments responsible for historic and ongoing crimes against children and humanity.

The original ITCCS federation was composed of groups from Ireland, England, the United States, Canada and Italy -

Templemore Forgotten Victims (Antrim, Ireland), The Friends and Relatives of the Disappeared (Canada), and the United against Church Terror (USA). By September, 2013, ITCCS had grown so popular that it has spread to twenty-six countries and with over fifty affiliated groups, which include prestigious Cult Ritual And Abuse Survivors' Organization (SMART) of the United States.

One of the most celebrated cases handled by ITCCS implicated Pope Francis. The news on Monday, October 28, 2013 has it this way: The criminal prosecution of yet another Pope can closer to reality this month as Italian Politicians agreed to work with the ITCCS in Common Law Court action against the papacy for its harboring of a wanted fugitive from justice: deposed Pope Benedict, Joseph Ratzinger.

The agreement came after a new eyewitness confirmed the involvement of Ratzinger in a ritual child sacrifice in Holland in August of 1987.

"I saw Joseph Ratzinger murder a little girl at French chateau in the fall of 1987," stated the witness, who was a regular participant in cult ritual torture and killing of children. "It was ugly and horrible, and it didn't happen just once. Ratzinger often took part. He and (Dutch Catholic Cardinal) Alfrink and (Bilderberger founder) Prince Bernhard were some of the more prominent men who took part."

This new witness confirms the account of Toos Nijenhuis, a Dutch woman who went public with eyewitness account of similar crimes, involving Ratzinger, Alfrink and Bernhard.

Soon after his historic resignation from the office of Catholic Pope on February 11, Joseph Ratzinger was convicted of crimes against humanity on February 25, 2013 by Brussels - based on International Common Law Court of Justice, and a global citizens arrest warrant was issued against him. Since then, he has evaded arrest within Vatican City under a decree of the present Pope Francis.

With the above case and so many cases both known and unknown, Satanism and cult religion has become the order of the day. Since most governments all over the world are implicated, it is becoming more and more difficult if not impossible to convict ritual killers like Ratzinger.

Researchers, especially the ones that are considered conspiracy theorists have offered series of proofs that establish the fact that so many American politicians and other prominent people are involved in cult regions. With their involvement in things that are opposed to the beliefs of the founding fathers, faulty policies relating to religions; education; security and other things are formulated to the detriment of the citizens.

The case study of a single mother who has seven children establishes this fact. It is again extracted from the book: Insanity Of Humanity which is as follows:

... One of the children who was a girl of about six years old started going to school one day. She found out that the teacher would not allow her to pray over her lunch as her mother have taught her.

The mother who did not even have a high school diploma pulled her out of school to home-school her and other children. This was the time home-schooling was not as popular as it is in the US. Back then, it was not official either and it was a subject of harassment from the school. The school bus would sit outside and lay on the horn every morning. The bus driver would yell, "truant" and sometimes even get out, going to bang the door. The school call all the time, and the mother stopped answering the phone.

One day, the mother got what she feared for a long time - an official letter saying she had to go to court for her daughter's truancy. She was dazed as she read the letter. She couldn't believe what she read, letting the letter fall out of her hand in despair. The daughter went to her and asked her if it was bad news. She said, "yes". She asked if she could read the letter. Since it was about her, she let her read the letter. Without her mother noticing it right away, the 6-year old girl got a red pen and began to circle several grammatical and spelling errors in the letter. Her mother scolded her, saying she wasn't supposed to do that to other people's papers. But then, the mother had done that to the girl's papers over times. So it was the mother that taught her at home.

When the mother went to court, taking the letter with her to make sure she went to the right place, she was bought before the judge. The Judge asked her if she knew why she was in the court. She handed him the letter, forgetting about the markings. She was almost certain that he would ask her a bunch of questions about her own education and concluded that she was unfit to home-school her daughter. He would, according to her conclusion, order her to take her daughter back to school.

When the Judge looked at the letter, he asked, "who put these markings on here?"

With apology, the mother told him it was the daughter in question.

The judge took off his glasses and looked at the letter again. He said to her, "well, the reason you're here today is that it is suspected that your daughter is not being properly educated. However, it appears that she is being educated, and from what I see here, it is clearly not coming from the public schools. This case is dismissed."

The mother did not realize that she had seen teaching her daughter 7th grade reading level instead of 1st grade.

This case indicates the fact that so many schools are established to show more interest in washing away traditional values and impacting global vision than in academics.

Also consider and juxtapose with the above case in the article that is also culled from the same book. It is as follows:

There is an article by Exhort-Ezine titled: "Should God's People Send Their Kids To Satan's School?" The article reads as follows:

"If Satan were to run a school, how would it run it?

"First - Satan would make an absolute law that no knowledge of the true God of the Bible can be taught. Not only could God not be talked to, He couldn't talk to anyone either. No prayers.

"Any religious teaching in Satan's schools must be about other gods.

"Second - in Satan's school, the basis of all instructions must be the religious belief that there is no Creator: that all creations happened by chance, that mankind was not special creation by God, that he is just one with the worms and monkeys. Evolution.

"Following this theory, Satan would teach that mankind is subject only to the same law as the worms and monkeys. Since we came from slime, we can act like slime. Unbridled breeding and sodomy are not sins, just different animal behaviors. In Satan's schools, ten commandment moralities *must never be imposed.*

"Third - Satan's schools must be chocked full of fruits of Satan's way of life - destructive sex, vicious fits of violence, and mind killing drugs. Such things as girls wearing skirts up to their butts and blouses down to their breasts. Or kids being able to get drugs more easily in the school halls than on the city streets. And mindless massacres, where young lives are blown to bits by other kids.

"Wait a minute - I have just described the American public schools. They are run just the way Satan would run a school. That means America public schools are Satan's school."

This writer may sound blunt but he was able to back up his points with cases and references to American Law and Government policies.

Before studying the means through which Satanism and Cult Religions are introduced to American society, it is important to note a few things about them.

Satanism, according to Wikipedia is a broad term referring to a group of western regions comprising diverse ideological and philosophical beliefs. Their shared features include symbolic association with, or admiration for the character of Satan or similar rebellious, promethean and, in their views liberating.

Again the excerpt that is made from the book: Satanism And Cult Religion which treats the issue extensively is as follows:

The name of "Satan" which connotes the terms "Satanism", "Satanic" and "Satanist" encompasses wide variety of ideological, philosophical and theological beliefs. Thus satanic groups or cults are quite different from one another although the use of the same terminologies still apply.

ReligionFacts attempts to classify satanic groups to help people understand what each believes and how each behaves. Not every group performs satanic rituals or participates in satanic worship or reads satanic bible or uses satanic symbols or attends the church of Satan that was established by Anton Szandor LaVey in 1966....

Also consider the following excerpts in the same book:

... It is instructive to note the followings about real Satanists:

44

1. *They dress and look normal. The long-term Satanist, according to Samuel Butler (an ex-Satanist), "has skeletons in their closet". The dangerous ones are not the Bikers or Gothic dressed or hippies or the ones with tattoos, green hair or body piercings. The dangerous ones are the clean cut looking Satanists, some highly placed with good jobs and careers like lawyers, policemen, clergy, media etc. So it is little wonder that Ratzinger was able to get to the position of Catholic Pope. Going by results of research works, there are countless number of Satanic Ritual Abuse (SRA) cases, especially sexual abuse cases among Catholic Priests. This invariably established the fact that Catholicism is fast becoming, if at all it has not become cult religion.*
2. *It should also be noted from this (Samuel Butler's) case study that the reasons for the missing of millions of people every year around the world can be attributed to satanic activities, using the least suspected places like Church, Temples, underground of private properties as places of sacrifices to Satan.*
3. *It is also instructive to note that Satanism can be practiced in various ways like religion, profession or career. It can be made public or in secret and spread through medium like media, business, religious or charity organizations. A good example is Lucis Trust, the leading and respectable Britain-based cult that worships Lucifer. The Lucis Trust ran a religious chapel at New York United Nations Headquarters called The Temple of Understanding. It was also originally founded as the Lucifer Trust in London in 1923. The Lucis Trust associated with UNO is the New York of the British organization. The name was changed from Lucifer Trust to Lucis Trust to make the nature of the organization less conspicuous. Some of the sponsors of the organization include Supreme Grand Commander of the Supreme Council, 33 Degree Southern District Scottish Rite Freemasons, The Rockefeller Foundation, The Marshal Field Family, The United Lodge of Theosophists of New York City and a host of others.*
4. *Satanism is practiced everywhere in the world with no country exempted. Its influence on mankind can never*

be quantified or overemphasized. The operations of Satanists like Luci Trust, Freemasons, Illuminati and countless of others have infused all aspects of life from generations to generations. Nearly every culture all over the world has one touch of Satanism or the other. The studies of the operation patterns of the media, politics, economy, social life and entertainments reveal that Satanism and cult religions have infiltrated the society through these means. These invariably condition the minds of the people to accept obscene things as entertainment materials, violence conduct as complementary of peace.

5. *The most effective weapons of Satanism are lies and deceptions although in some cases they use threats to get people to comply with their instructions. Typical Satanists will go extra miles to win people's trust.* (Perhaps this explains reason Lucifer Trust was changed to Lucis Trust.) *They probably suspect most people would not want to trust Lucifer who has bad reputation as contender with God, going by what the Bible says about him. Satanists always claim to be concerned about humanity. They create flashy things or scheme spectacular events to catch attentions...*

Faulty External And Internal Affair Policies

This aspect is the final and crucial topic to be treated because it actually influences many nations to be hostile towards Americans, going the results of research works.

Thomas Jefferson pointed the need to be at peace with other nations when he said, *"Peace and friendship with all mankind is our wisest policy, and I wish we may be permitted to pursue it."* George Washington also prayed, *"...Bless, O Lord, the whole race of mankind and let the world be filled with the knowledge of Thee and Thy Son, Jesus Christ."* The modern United States had became a nation that creates evils and civil wars in countries where there is modest peace. Reason for this always boils on dominating world politics and economy. With its military and other strengths, the United States becomes world police and bully that always takes it upon itself to remove leaders in weaker nations at will and impose their choice on them. This is done by raising and equipping rebels that will cause civil wars, according to research works.

The following excerpts are made from the author's book, titled: Africans In Bondage - A Collection Of Academic Paper Presentations In Drama Book One And Two:

DR T. A: ... *Having established these two points, let's now consider the source of Ebola Virus. Ebola Virus according to research works is made by the US scientists in deliberate attempt to spread the deadly disease across some West African nations, killing thousands of Africans at its peak in 2014. Professor Frances A. Boyle, a respected scholar of bio-warfare and international law at the University of Illinois first made his astounding discovery. He said that what we are dealing with here is a biological warfare work that was conducted at bio-warfare laboratories set up by the USA on the West Coast of Africa. If you look at a map produced by Centers for Disease Control and Prevention, you can see where these laboratories are located. They are across the heart of Ebola epidemic at the West Coast of Africa. The Professor also said that he had proof that the Pentagon had ordered the COC to test biological weapons in Sierra Leone as early as 1988. Dr. Paul Craig Roberts, former Assistant Secretary to the Treasure for Economic Policy in the U.S asked whether the U. S government is the "greatest master of criminal of our time." Going by the diseases that are researched, biological agents that are used as biological weapons such as Bird flu; Dengue fever; Lassa fever; Anthrax; Marbury Virus; HIV/AIDS, the answer is not farfetched. While we may not consider the Western Nations as enemies, we definitely cannot consider them as friendly nations....*

... The case study of Bakassi (the oil rich area in dispute between Nigeria and Cameroon) *and so many other cases prove to us that there are some warmongering nations who want developing or under developed nations to go into wars. This issue boils on the same question of why are these nations doing this? Results of research works indicate that nations with wealth or natural resources always fall victims of these warmongering nations. If your country is wealthy but weak militarily, you are in trouble.*

Only time will tell when these warmongers will come to your country and cause trouble. Unless of course you make the so-called "almighty" countries like the United States and a handful of them your allies, you are alone in the midst of wolfs that want pounds of your flesh in their bellies. The investigations into the cause of civil wars in counties like Syria, Iraq and many others revealed the fact that conflicts are all about powers, not necessarily within the conflicts areas but outside. Any government which, as I indicated earlier, falls out of favour with warmongering nations is always faced with civil wars. More often than not, it is always difficult to really find out why a country is full of rebels. Sometimes there are as many as five different versions of rebels involved in conflicts in one country. All of them are usually well armed to harm themselves and wreck the country to exhaustion with steady supply of ammunition. Thanks to the warmongering nations who always ensure that the rebels are never in short supply of ammunition.

The warmongering nations invaded Iraq and destroy the country. What eventually came out of the plight of the country was oil trade with the military force of the warmongers protecting smuggling operations and illegal exports of the natural resources.

In the Russian President press conference in December, 2015, it was revealed that when an Islamic anti-ISIS coalition was established, people did not know that there was also NATO-led coalition and the Russian-Syrian coalition. It turned out to be that there were three coalitions against ISIS. The Russian President asked a very disturbing question: "is it really so difficult to deal with this evil? Maybe there are some other goals and some other plans here. May be it is not ISIS problem." To substantiate this suspicion, the Russian defense ministry revealed the picture of 11,000 oil trucks that were taking away the country's oil in Iraq. Similar thing happened in Syria at the time the country was getting ravaged with war. While referring to the creation and excess of Islamic terrorists, the Russian President quoted the US President Reagan, saying "Somoza may be a son of a bitch, but he is our son of a bitch."

All the results of research works on wars in most, if not all conflict areas in the world all boil on the issues of both the world economic and political dominance...

Vladimir Vladimirovich Putin, the President of the Russian Federation said in a plea for caution to the US in New York Times, 12 September, 2013, *"It is extremely dangerous to encourage people to see themselves as exceptional, whatever the motivation. There are big countries and small countries, rich and poor, those with long democratic traditions and those still finding their way to democracy. Their policies differ, too. We are all different, but when we ask for the Lord's blessings, we must not forget that God created us equal...*

"... Recent events surrounding Syria have prompted me to speak directly to the American people and their political leaders. It is important to do so at the same time of insufficient communication between societies. Relation between us have passed through different stages. We stood against each other during cold war. But we were also allies once, and defeated the Nazis together. The universal international organization - the United Nations - was then established to prevent such devastation from ever happening again.

"It is alarming that military intervention in internal conflicts in foreign countries has become commonplace for the United States. Is it in America's long-term interest? I doubt it. Millions around the world increasingly see America not as a model democracy but as relying solely on brute force, cobbling coalition together under the slogan 'you're either with us or against us...'

"No matter how targeted the strikes or how sophisticated the weapons, civilian casualties are inevitable, including the elderly and children, whom the strikes are meant to protect...

"We must stop using the language of force and return to the path of civilized diplomatic and political settlement."

The Russian President also said in an interview, *"The U. S is a very democratic state. There's no doubt about that. And it originally developed as a democratic state. When the first settlers set their foot on the continent, life forced them to forge a relationship and maintain dialogue with each other to survive. That's why America was conceived as a fundamental democracy."*

CONCLUSION:
Restoration Of American Value System To Its Original Shape

For the United States to remain vibrant and great, its value system which was constructed by the founding fathers and which is getting eroded by tyrants who often pose as politicians, philanthropists, financiers and so many others who are respected in the society must be restored to its original shape. These tyrants have gone too far in eroding the American Value System right before the days of Andrew Jackson. They know very well that the best way to destroy a nation is to first erode the value system, which not only sanction anyone who does not fit into the system but also boost the moral values of the people.

The Bible says in Proverb 25: 5, *"Take away the wicked from before the king, And his throne will be established in righteousness."*

As pointed earlier, the erosion of the value system creates hostile environments in streets, schools, even at homes and other places in the U. S through various means like music that celebrate obscenities, cartoons that pass subliminal messages to the subconscious minds of children, movies and computer games that promote violence. If all these items that are responsible for violence and obscenities in the society are not rid of or curbed by committed people in the positions of influence, installing sanity into the American society will take lots of major miracles.

Other means that are used to erode the American Value System as also pointed out are: politics, education, cult religions and media, including social media.

It is a long way to bring back to shape the American Value System as originally constructed by the founding fathers. Obviously, it will take lots of efforts of committed people to educate and inform the U. S citizens of the dire need to restore the system.

It is the hope of the author that the materials in this book are resourceful and helpful enough to inspire or wake up the giants in the United States to man up their responsibilities to the nation, their families and fellow citizens. If it has inspired or informed anyone or everyone of the implications of getting the value system completely eroded, there is need for politicians or scholars or Christian or community leaders or school teachers or parents and even students to do something about bringing it back to its original shape. If there is anytime the United States needs its citizens to rescue the nation from tyrants, it is now. Just as John F. Kennedy said, every good citizen of the United States must think of what to do to save the country instead of thinking of what to get from it.

THE STORIES AND STUDIES OF AFRICAN VALUES

*The 26 Stories And Studies Of Value Systems That Are
Peculiar To African Nations*

Most African and other nations often build and develop their economic, social, political and other structures at the expense of their Value Systems which are often constructed by the prevailing norms, cultures, law and order in the societies.

The Value System in each country is always the live wire that powers other vital structures, including security machinery. Thus it is possible to have security challenges in a country with good political structure and healthy economy. In order to reinforce their Value Systems, some countries embed what the nations stand for and against in their National Anthems and The Pledge to the nations.

The neglect or shutting down of National Value Systems in most African nations give rooms for vices and crimes to be on the increase.

This book is designed to be studied by parents, teachers and students in primary or junior and high schools in Africa with the objectives of imbibing African traditional and moral values into them. With particular focus on children and youths, through the use of stories; poems; proverbs; quotes and class activities, the author attempts to give vivid pictures of African Values as opposed to westernization which is clearly wiping out what the founding fathers of the nations on the continent stand for.

THE AFRICAN VALUES AND LEGACIES

*The Studies On African Value Systems With Analysis And Use
Of Quotes And Proverbs That Depict The Pains, Struggles and
Sufferings In Africa Nations*

Results of research works reveal that any nation that fails to orientate all categories of its citizens on what the country stands for and against gives rooms for other countries to devalue the national value, violate the law and order; deforming the prevailing norms and cultures in all the communities.

Most of African values, enriched with proverbs like "a goat is never pronounced innocent if the judge is a leopard" and "when brothers fight to death; a stranger inherits their father's estate", are getting eroded with westernization. The African heritages through

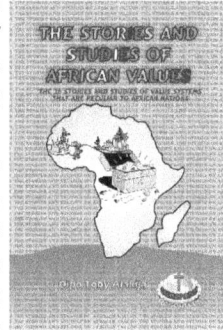

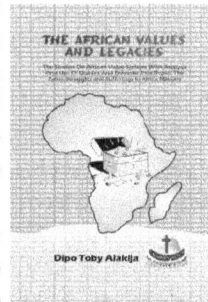

52

the transfer of cultures, norms and order from one generation to another are threatened with extinctions since the time of colonization, particularly in oil-rich African nations.

The shutting down of value systems which are usually designed to boost moral values of citizens and enhance the functions of political, social and economic machineries are responsible for civil wars, terrorism, genocides and other atrocities in most African nations.

This book which is designed to be studied in African Tertiary Institutions shares the results of research works into the causes of conflicts, political and economic servitude in Africa; using the analyses of quotes of some of the notable leaders and African proverbs to reinforce the value systems on the continent.

SPOIL THE CHILD, DESTROY THE NATION

A Collection Of Sixteen Educational Dramas That Depict The Compromised Nigerian Values

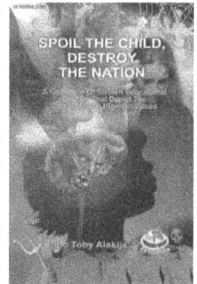

This collection of sixteen short educational dramas exemplifies the decadent lifestyles, especially among Nigerian youths as opposed to the family and national values that are portrayed in the pledge to the nation.

All the stories are based on some of the most intriguing cases that are studied at different times and locations in Nigeria.

While some dramas hold westernization through means of information and entertainments accountable for the near extinction of the major part of Nigerian values, others establish the fact that parents who spare their children from rigours of normal life often create out of them menaces that would pose serious threats to lives and properties in future. This parental factor also exposes young minds to life of luxuries instead of preparing them to face the huddles ahead of them.

The various issues that boil on the sources of social vices and crimes in Nigeria are so vividly presented in all the dramas that they can be imagined like motion pictures.

AFRICANS IN BONDAGE

A Selection Of Academic Paper Presentations With Nine Studied Cases In Drama Book One Titled: "African Nations Still In Fetters" And A Collection Of Eight Stories Of The Spirit Eyes In Drama Book Two Titled: "The Spiritual Bondage"

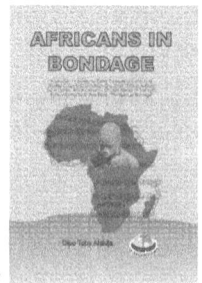

BOOK ONE: AFRICANS STILL IN FETTERS

Patrice Emery Lumumba, Congo's First Prime Minister and President said at All-African Conference in 1960, "The Colonialists care for

53

nothing for Africa for her own sake. They are attracted by African riches and their actions are guided by the desire to preserve their interests in Africa against the wishes of the African people. For colonialists all means are good if they help them to possess these riches."

An African adage says; "if you close your eyes to facts, you will learn through accidents."

The above and so many other quotes which are used as emphases on the results of research works into the claims of some notable African leaders indicate that Western Nations are not as friendly as they seem right from the time of slave trade.

The playwright attempts to present the results of his research works on why African nations are never free from conflicts, economic, social and political servitude through the use of different academic papers that are treated in educational dramas with the titles "Grand Conspiracies Against Africa", "The Speeches Of Discord", "The Conspiracy Theory Of History", "The Brain Development Of A Child", "The Problem With Technology", "The Handover Of Legacy", "The Warmongering Nations", "The Slave Masters In Africa" and "Mothers: The Determinants Of Destinies" in book one.

BOOK TWO: SPIRITUAL BONDAGE

With studied cases that are peculiar to Africa, the author attempts to explain some mysteries relating to cultism; witchcraft; black magic and others. These dramas titled: "The Threats Of Cult Members On Campus", The Choice Of Death", "Lagidi: The Spirit Husband", "The Mirage Of A Marriage", "Truth Is The Weapon Of Freedom", "The Enemies Of Marriage", "The Wrath Of An Accuser" and "House Of God In A Mess" are mostly based on real life experiences. They paint vivid pictures of how the spirit realm can influence the physical world.

BUILDING YOUR FUTURE AS YOUNG AFRICANS
A Success And Nation Building Course Handbook

Going by world history, mankind is always faced with all kinds of challenges that are peculiar to each nation but the patriotic or unpatriotic attitudes of the citizens always determine if the country would overcome the problems or not.

Many African youths who see and feel the problems in their countries sometimes blame the Governments. Consequently, a lot of them are enlisted as rebels who often times fight against their Governments. They are also involved in crimes, terrorism and other

atrocities without realizing their deadly implications in future.

Youths are often ignorant of the fact that what they do today will determine what their tomorrow and the future of their countries would be.

This book makes serious attempts to help both youths and adults in Africa to understand the normal process of real success through the resource materials inside.

The author explains how problems can be seen as opportunities to excel in life, using real life stories as cases for studies, quoting relevant authorities to buttress his points.

The book is also designed to teach African youths of the need to build their nations by encouraging them to enhance their values through skill acquisitions, setting goals and making best use of their potentials and the available resources.

THE REDEEMER AND THE DRAGON
Aa Epic Of Three Kingdoms

Dragon, the king of Doom kingdom gets the legal right to rule over the kingdom of man when First Couple breaks the Law Of Dominion and turns all the mortals into his slaves. When The Father who creates all the kingdoms sends The Redeemer to deliver them, Brethren is selected as one of the few giant warriors that will terrorize Dragon and the rulers of darkness in the decisive battle between Eternity kingdom and Doom kingdom over eternal destinations of the people.

Because The Redeemer counts on the mortal warriors called Believers to deliver the rest of the slaves, he equips them with The Word and Comforter who teaches them all things. However, a warrior of Dragon called Ignorance blindfolds vast majority of the people and makes them oblivious of the battlefields in The Flesh, The Mind and The Spirit. Since most of these mortals cannot see beyond their immediate environments, the enemies get the chance to lead them on the path of Doom kingdom which is a place of eternal agony, making the battle on the way to Eternity kingdom of The Father so fierce that only the violent Believers can get to the place.

THE WEIGHT OF DEATH
A Collection Of The Stories Of The Spirit Eyes

PLAY ONE: HORROR IN THE FAMILY: Talimi probably did not envisage his death when he was trying to compel his son, Damola to succeed him in the occult Brotherhood. Other members of the secret cult were aware of the battle between them. So when Talimi died; his family, especially Damola who was a diehard Christian

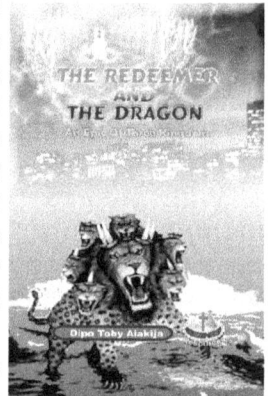

began to fall prey to the cult. Using all their powers and the spirit that posed as Talimi's ghost, the cult waged war against the family, tormenting and making the members to be at loggerheads.

PLAY TWO: RITUAL KIDS' KIDNAPPERS: Victor and the rest of the members of the School Bible Club were taught that there are lots of evil people in this world but he did not understand why God allowed him to be among the children that were taken away from their parents. He soon understood that he was to be used by God to rescue other children who did not know that everyone that truly believes in Jesus has the power to overcome evil.

PLAY THREE: THE WEIGHT OF DEATH: Awoseun would not have known the real source of problems of mankind if his father had not given him the power to see demons tormenting the people in different ways. What he was yet to know, however, was the power of light over darkness. When he was caught in crossfire between these powers, he desperately sought for deliverance.

THE YOUNG GENERATION STORY BOOK

The 26 Stories That Depict The Values Of The National Anthem And The Pledge To Nigeria In Relation With The Value system

An adage says that a man who builds a house without building his children only builds what the children will later sell. Similarly, a nation that builds its economy and political structures without putting the national values into considerations builds what the citizens will later destroy. Plutarch said, "the richest soil, uncultivated produces the rankest weeds." This probably explains reasons the rich soil (natural and other resources) in Nigeria produces the rankest weeds in the forms of social vices and crimes.

Nigerians pay too much attention on politics, economy and other things at the expense of the value system that is embedded in the national anthem and the pledge to the nation. Because of the near extinctions of moral; family and traditional values with the belief in God Of Creation, the abundant resources in Nigeria had become snares for the citizens who are supposed to use them for the good of the present and future generations.

This book which is designed for Primary and Junior Secondary School Students teaches the values of the national anthem and the pledge to Nigeria through the use of 26 stories, poems and class activities; some of which are selected from the author's books

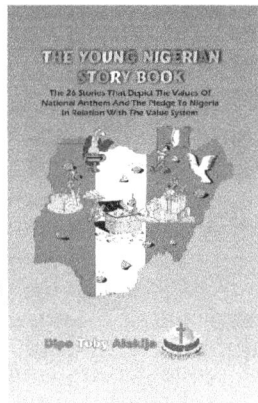

titled Foundation and Young Generation Bible Club Story Books. With each of the stories titled with a line or a topic in the anthem and the pledge, the book teaches young minds civic responsibilities and moral lessons some of which are viewed from Christian perspectives, serving as reminders of the purposes of the national anthem and the pledge to Nigeria.

CHRISTIAN BASIC MINISTRIES AND LEADERSHIP COURSE BOOK

As it is a common saying that the hood does not make a monk, the dignified positions and bogus titles of many Christian leaders in modern days do not really make them Gospel Ministers.

This course book - a compilation of five resource materials on Successful Christianity, Christian Basic Ministries, Christian Leadership, Christian Education Methodology and Ministries Of Improvisions - aims at making every matured Christian an effective minister and leader at their respective homes, communities and nations. It teaches various ways Christians can meet up to their responsibilities and commitments as ministers and leaders that reconcile people to God and edify the Body Of Christ, reaching out to souls through available means.

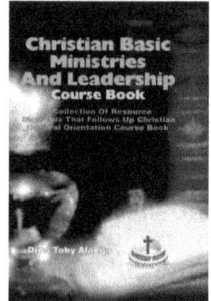

All of the resource materials are in use in Bible Colleges, Churches and other ministries to raise Christian workers, Evangelists, Missionaries and other Ministers that will serve at various levels and capacities.

FOOTSTEPS IN THE MUD

The Drama Package Of Results Of Research Works That trace Global And Societal Vices To The Corrupt Or Lost Of Family Values

The 13-Episode drama book involves Bosede who learnt many wrong things from her parents' conduct and foul language. She was forced to marry Kola when she became pregnant. Using her mother's method to handle her father, she tried to subject Kola to her control. In the course of that, she made life terrible for him. Although her mother tried to warn her of the implications of maltreating her husband but Bosede has grown out of control. Consequently, while looking for peace, Kola was pushed out of the house. He made friends with some guys who taught him the unholy ways of life and influenced him to become a menace in the house.

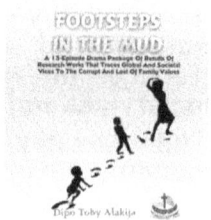

Junior who was born at time the couple never proved to be responsible parents also learnt wrong things from them. He decided to follow his father's footsteps by taking alcohol when he was in primary school. As if that was not bad enough, he tried to teach other children in the school the madness in his home. A school teacher, however, was able to influence him and his mother by teaching them Christian morals. Even then, Junior was soon caught in the crossfire at home as his father tried to enlist him as a future member of a secret cult that posed as a social club.

CHRISTIAN COMMUNICATIONS AND HUMAN RESOURCES

The world is not in need of those who will fix errors of humanity but in dire need of matured Christians that would use their gifts to communicate the word of God and lead their families, the Church, communities and their countries in the way of righteousness. Very few of them, however, seem to have what it takes to take their positions as leaders and ministers in their spheres despite their God-given potentials. Thus this Course Book - a compilation of five resource materials on Christian Oral Communications, Christian Drama Communications, Christian Musical Communications, Christian Human Resources and Children Evangelism - makes serious attempts to introduce everybody into various creative ministries that are required in the Body of Christ and in the world. It teaches in a simple manner the management of human resources and the ways Christians can use their gifts to reach out to souls through speaking, writing, drama, media, musical and children ministries. The resource materials equip and help individuals to identify their callings, providing Biblical principles and guidelines on how to be effective and productive in the service of the Lord in spite of the hostile environments.

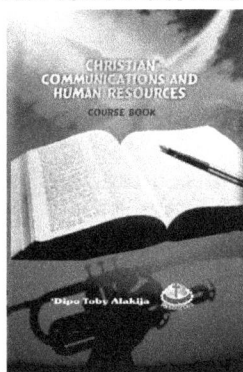

INSANITY OF HUMANITY

The Results Of Research Works Into Various Methods Of Brainwashing

Man is made to exercise his freewill. The mind of his own and the power to choose between right and wrong, good and evil, light and darkness is about to be washed away through brainwashing. The agents of control dubbed as Secret Government by John Todd (the top Illuninati defector) have put necessary machinery in place to ensure that all human beings are in conformity in their thinking and ways of life, trying to wipe away diversity, which makes each person unique.

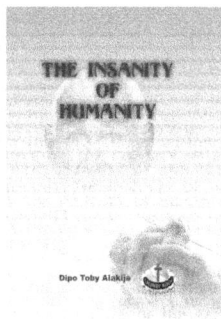

This book attempts to shed light on how the techniques of mind control are applied through the use of propaganda, education, entertainments, drugs, religions, media and other means of communications. It is the result of research works, some of which are based on findings of various researchers and writers like Bugger Lugz, Edward Hunter, Hadley Cantril, Herbert Krugman, David L. Robb, Vaughan Bell, Juliana Gomez, Ryan Duffy Vice, Henry Makow, David Nicholls, Fritz Springmeire, Steven Hassan, Renate Thienel, Debra Pursell, Mary Pride and a host of others who are acknowledged in this book.

NO MORE TEARS TO SHED

Kidnappers took Tokunbo away from his grand parents in a city in Nigeria when he was a little boy. A nice woman found him in another town and gave him a false identity. She spoilt him with love, making him to grow into a rebellious teenager that was not appreciated anywhere. When Janet made him a Christian, however, life began to make sense to him until the day he was beaten to the point of death for the offence he knew nothing about. He left the town for the city which, unknown to him, held his true identity and the link to his parents in the United States. To find them was only a question of time.

THE UNROMANTIC LOVE BIRDS
And other short stories about love and marriages

They were very much in love right from their school days but when they got married and had children, romance became the game Charles' wife refused to play. No matter how much he tried to make her understand the unbearable condition her unromantic attitude has subjected him into, she would not change. Consequently, after enduring for so long, he was forced to look for the women that would make up for her weakness. He unofficially married a beautiful lady of insane jealousy. Though she was ready to give him what was missing in his marriage, it soon dawn on him that he has solved one big problem only to create a bigger one.

THE BATTLE OF THE CONQUERORS

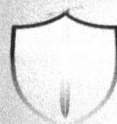

Wickedness takes over the land of Bondage from First Couple and subjects everybody into slavery without giving anybody the chance to be free. Love brings The Redeemer from Eternity and offers the slaves the chance to escape. Wickedness soon declares war and engages everyone in the battle. The Redeemer makes the redeemed people Conquerors by giving them the armour of war and Comforter but Wickedness cannot be undone. He has several thousands of years of experience in the

59

through the media, music, publications, films, conduct and foul language; making them to lose their moral and family values.

This book one just like the rest of other volumes is an attempt to bring back moral instructions into schools and campuses through the use of stories, hymn tuned songs, poems, Bible lessons and class activities. It is designed to assist teachers and ministers in Secondary Schools, Bible Clubs, Churches and Campus Fellowships to teach people, especially youths the Word of God and serves as a school text book in subjects relating to literature, music and other creative works.

FOUNDATION BIBLE CLUB A-Z STORY BOOK
Volume 1 With 26 Stories, 26 Bible
Lessons, 26 Rhymes And 26 Songs For Book For Young Minds

An adage says, "a man who builds a house without building his child builds what the child will later sell." Proverbs 22:6 says, "train up a child in the way he should go: and when he is old, he will not depart from it." This book is an attempt to assist parents and teachers to meet up to the challenges that befall them in carrying out this important function in the light of the moral decadence that is prevailing all over the world.

The first edition of the book was used by several thousands of teachers, ministers and parents in schools, Churches and homes to build the moral values of young ones. Apart from the stories, songs and Bible passages for the young ones to study, there is a seminar material that is based on the lecture which the author delivered to school proprietors, children ministers and Christian professionals in this volume.

THE YOUNG GENERATION BIBLE CLUB STORY BOOK
Volume 2 Of Foundation Bible Club A-Z Story Book For Young Minds

Although this book serves as a follow-up to the stories and lessons in All Generations Story Book or Foundation Bible Club A-Z Story Book, it is a separate academic, evangelical and missionary tool to reach out and teach young ones in primary and junior high schools. Just like other volumes, it contains stories, songs, poems, Bible lessons and class activities that can be used by parents and teachers at homes, Sunday Schools, School Bible Clubs and other Fellowships. It is a manual that assists them in boosting the moral values of children of all age groups in the modern days that are characterized with brainwashing information, ungodly teaching materials and entertainments.

Apart from the contents for the young ones, there are also

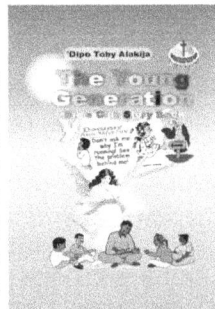

war. So he is quick to recognize the weakness of the redeemed people who are ignorant of their strengths and advantages. Although the Conquerors fight like immutable giants, rescuing victims of war, many people suffer heavy casualties.

Since King Wickedness knows that a redeemed person is strong enough to chase one thousand of his warriors at a time, and two would put ten thousand into flight, he enlists as one of his warriors the people's deadliest enemy called Disunity.

Wickedness is able to strike the people by making them to fight with one another, turning what is supposed to be their best moments in the battle into tales of woes.

BLOODSHED IN CAMPUS
Novel And Play Edition

A poor widow tearfully warned her son, Richard, against joining the bad gang when he got an admission into one of the Nigerian Universities. He resisted the membership of groups of students, including the Christian Fellowship until he had an encounter with a member of The Black Skulls - a deadly and ruthless secret cult on the campus.

Before Richard knew what he was up against, the head of The Black Skulls had arranged items for his initiation into the cult. While resisting being initiated, he ran to the Christian Fellowship for help. The leader of the Christian Fellowship dragged The President of Students' Union Government (S.U.G) into the conflict. With the involvement of the S.U.G President, another formidable cult called The Red Eyes felt obliged to team up against The Black Skulls. Then the campus turned into a battlefield and BLOODSHED became the order of the black day.

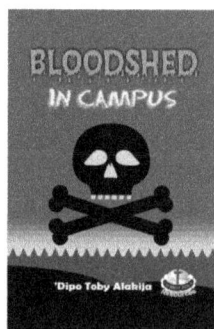

NETWORK BIBLE CLUB
YOUTH AND ADULT BOOK ONE
A collection of 26 life transforming stories, 26 poems, 26 hymn tuned songs and weekly Bible lessons

The issue of moral instructions in schools and at homes is threatened with extinction. Consequently, so many youths are involved in prostitution, drug addictions, cultism, fraudulent practices, armed robberies and other crimes. Those who are supposed to be trained as leaders in various walks of life are the ones posing serious threats to many lives. Many parents who fail to add moral values to the upbringing of their children often times breed potential criminals under their roofs without knowing it. Apart from these, many other people negatively influence young ones

lectures and tips on how to effectively use the book to raise God fearing children. All the published volumes of the book are in use by thousands of teachers, ministers and parents worldwide.

RANSOM FOR LOVE

She accepted his marriage proposal without knowing the kind of person he was. She soon discovered that he was a mean and ruthless guy who was always ready to get whatever he wanted by all means even if he has to pay for it with the lives of others. She was in his bondage, especially when her parents who believed he was a generous and gentleman were on his side.

Because she considered the proposal to marry him as a marriage engagement with the devil incarnate, she decided that she would rather die than to share her life with him. Then out of the blues, this passionate gentleman sneaked into her life despite all she did to discourage him. She could not resist his love for her when he offered to set her free from the devil incarnate. Then the battle began – sooner than they anticipated.

THE YOUNG GHANAIAN STORY BOOK

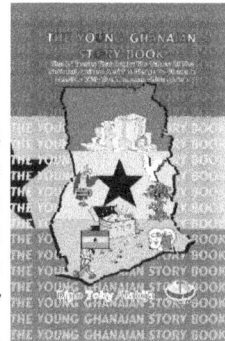

The 26 Stories That Depict The Values Of The National Anthem And The Pledge To Ghana In Relation With The Ghanaian Value System

An African adage says that a man who builds a house without building his children only builds what the children will later sell. Similarly, a nation that builds its economy and political structures without putting the National Value into serious considerations builds what the citizens will later destroy. Plutarch said, "the richest soil, uncultivated produces the rankest weeds." This probably explains reasons the rich soil (natural and other resources) in some African countries produces the rankest weeds in the forms of social vices and crimes.

To cultivate Ghanaian rich soil, people in the positions of influence such as parents; school teachers; political and other leaders need to invest a lot of their time and resources in grooming young minds into responsible and reasonable citizens. Thus investing much resources on politics, economy and other things at the expense of raising future leaders is a great risk which no country can afford to take.

This book which is designed for Primary and Junior Secondary School Students teaches National Values that are embedded in The

National Anthem and The Pledge To Ghana through the use of 26 stories, poems and class activities; some of which are selected from the author's books titled Foundation and Young Generation Bible Club Story Books. With each of the stories titled with a line or a topic in the anthem and the pledge, the book teaches young minds civic responsibilities and moral lessons some of which are viewed from Christian perspectives, serving as reminders of the purposes of the National Anthem and The Pledge To Ghana.

THE VALUES OF THE ANTHEMS AND THE PLEDGE TO NIGERIA

Comparative Studies Of Old, New National Anthems And The Pledge To Nigeria In Relation With The Value System

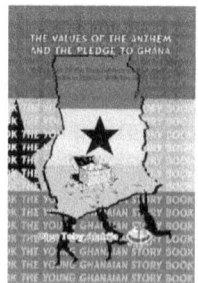

Out of sheer arrogance or ignorance or negligence, most political leaders in the past and present have violated the oaths they took before they assumed offices. This probably explains reasons most Nigerian citizens have failed to fulfil the pledges they made to their country when they were in schools. Since Government comes and goes, the people who would remain need not allow anything to tamper with the value systems which are embedded in the National Anthem and The Pledge To Nigeria. Most citizens, especially youths do not realize that failures to fulfil their pledges to the nation is breaking part of either Criminal or Civil Law. Consequently, malpractices that range from cheating during the examination to electoral fraud seem to have grown into bacteria that kill the patriotic spirits within Nigerian Value System. The bacteria also give births to vices and crimes which are the causes of social, economic and political catastrophes in the society.

This book which is designed to be studied by both youths and adults provides insights into the National Value System and attempts to interpret the meanings of the two anthems and the pledge to Nigeria. Through their interpretations, the author also gives vivid pictures of the things that are intended to characterize the people as responsible and reasonable citizens of Nigeria at the earliest stage of their lives.

.THE VALUES OF THE ANTHEM AND THE PLEDGE TO GHANA

The Studies Of The National Anthem And The Pledge To Ghana In Relation With The Value System

In order to encourage Ghanaian citizens to man up to their responsibilities, Dr Kwame Nkrumah said; "countrymen, the task ahead is great indeed, and heavy is the responsibility; and yet it is a noble and glorious challenge - a challenge which calls for the courage to believe, the courage to dare, the courage to do, the courage to envision, the courage to fight, the courage to achieve the highest excellencies and fullness greatness of man. Dare we ask for more?" The analysis of this quote in line with the National Anthem and The Pledge To Ghana proves that the Ghanaian Value System is well built on a very solid foundation. However, out of sheer arrogance or ignorance or negligence, many people in the positions of influence have violated the pledges they made to the country. Most citizens, especially youths do not realize that failures to fulfil their pledges to the nation is breaking part of either Criminal or Civil Law. Consequently, malpractice that range from cheating during the examination to electoral fraud seem to have grown into bacteria that can kill the patriotic spirits within most Value Systems in Africa. The bacteria equally give birth to vices and crimes which are the causes of social, economic and political catastrophes in most African nations.

This book which is designed to be studied by both youths and adults provides insights into the Ghanaian National Value System and attempts to interpret the meanings of The Anthem and The Pledge To Ghana. Through their interpretations, the author also gives vivid pictures of the things that are intended to characterize the people as responsible and reasonable citizens of Ghana at the earliest stage of their lives.

SATANISM AND CULT RELIGIONS
The Studies Of Satanic Strongholds In Relation With Missing People Who Are Used As Ritual Sacrifices

With historic resignation of Joseph Ratzinger, the deposed Pope Benedict who was convicted of crimes against humanity, it becomes evident that Satanism is mingled with Christianity and so many other religions. High profile members of some respectable Christian denominations, charity, character-building and other organizations are implicated in the practice of Satanism and cult religions.

Satanism and cult religions have also infiltrated all areas of life; including world politics, economy, education, different cultures, laws and social orders.

With various studied cases like the association of UNO with Lucis Trust which was once known as Lucifer Trust in 1923, results of research works prove that Satanism and cult religions are both strongholds that are used to subdue nations all over the world with exception of none.

This book makes serious attempts to expose some of these

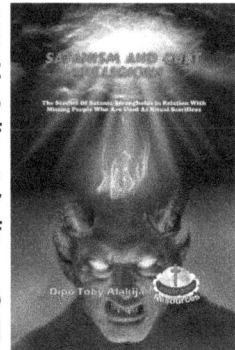

strongholds, proving the facts that the official reports about missing people and the discoveries of mass graves of school children in many areas are all governments' efforts to cover up truths about human ritual sacrifices that are taking place everywhere in the world.

SUCCESSFUL CHRISTIANITY AND BASIC MINISTRIES
A Collection Of Resource Materials That Precedes Christian Ministries And Basic Leadership Course Book

The first question is how Christianity is practiced even in a hostile environment. Next to that is the question about the potentials of Christians in spite of their apparent limitations. The other issues are connected to the successes, deliverance, callings, basic ministries of all Christians and evangelism. Various schools of thoughts have attempted these questions but many answers only portray Christianity as a form of religion instead of a way of life as specified by God. Some answers give room for compromise, hypocrisies, dogmas and denominational doctrines. The misconceptions about these areas of Christianity have brought about worldliness instead of righteousness and false achievements instead of fulfillment.

This book which contains six different subjects had been used to hold seminars at various levels, train ministers and Christian workers in Bible Schools and to equip the Church. It explains in simple terms the seemingly complex issues on practice of Christianity, Potentials, Deliverance, God's Kind Of Success, Evangelism and Basic Ministries of a Christian with Biblical principles, life transforming stories and illustrations.

All These And Other Books Are Distributed Worldwide And Published By The Publishing House Of
Calvary Rock Resources
19, Ajina Street, Ikenne-Remo,
Ogun - State, Nigeria
Web Site: www.calvaryrock.org

www.ingramcontent.com/pod-product-compliance
Lightning Source LLC
Chambersburg PA
CBHW032120280326
41933CB00009B/930